CALLED TO BE SAINTS

I Corinthians 1:2

FAY ELLIS BUTLER, Ph.D.

CALLED TO BE SAINTS

All Rights Reserved
Copyright © by Fay Ellis Butler
ISBN 1-883483-00-X

Second Printing
Printed in the United States of America
Published by ELLIS-BUTLER MINISTRIES
P.O. Box 330702
Stuyvesant Station
Brooklyn, New York 11233-=0008

Dedicated
to
My Parents,
Two dedicated servants of God,
who have gone on to be with the Lord.

RALPH NATHANIEL ELLIS, SR.
and
BEATRICE RICKS ELLIS

TABLE OF CONTENTS

Preface	i
Glossary	ii
Introduction	1
Made in the Image of God	7

    'Soul' defined, 7.
    'Spirit of man' defined, 8.
    'Body' defined, 10.
    'Will' defined, 12.

A New Creation   15

    'Fruits' Worthy of repentance, 17.
    A contrite and humble spirit, 18.
    The willingness to repent to God, 19
    The willingness to repent to others, 20
    The willingness to forgive, 20.
    The willingness to forgive yourself, 25.

The Mind Game   29

    The mind defined (conscious, subconscious, unconscious), 29.
    Satan cannot read your mind, 30.
    The 'spirit of torment', 32.
    'Flashbacks' and healing 'the pain of the memory', 33.
    Closing 'doorways', 37.
    Resisting the devil, 39.
    Deceptions and Devices, 41.

Sanctification: A Lifetime Process   49

    'Laying aside weights', 52.
    'Laying aside sin', 53.
    'Neither give place to the devil', 55.

'Keeping your tongue', 55.
The Word Sanctifies, 58.
The Holy Ghost sanctifies, 59.
The Holy Ghost does not work in the presence of sin, 61.

Weapons Against the Enemy 65

The Blood of Jesus, 66.
The Holy Ghost, 72.
The Word of God, 78.
The Name of Jesus, 84.
Prayer and Intercession, 90.
Praise and Worship, 100.
Speaking in an unknown Tongue, 105.
Self-Examination #4, 106.

How to Know the Will of God For My Life 107

'Proving the acceptable Will of God, 109.
The 'Fruit of the Spirit' manifested, 114.
'Fruit' harvested, 117.
The Power of God manifested, 118.
When will I know I am in the Will of God, 118.

Conclusion 121

Appendix 125

I   The Tongue's Diversity, 125.
II   The Complexity of The Heart, 126.
III   Scripture Memorization Plan, 127.
IV   Descriptive Names of Jesus, 128.
V   The Lord's Prayer, An Analysis, 129.
VI   An Annual Self-Evaluation, 130.
VII   Tripartite Nature of Man (Diagram) 132,133

Bibliography 134

Other Books by the Author

PREFACE

God has instructed me to write in order to supplement the teaching ministries of the Body of Christ. In the early 1980s, during a Soul Winner's Convention with Evangelist John David Lawrence in Atlanta, Georgia, the Lord spoke through him while he was praying for me, with the instructions, "Write, Write for my people". I did not begin to write immediately, but as I began to travel and minister in conventions, revivals and retreats, the needs of God's people became my source of inspiration and revelation to write. Therefore, *I WRITE*. Most of the time it is not difficult because the Holy Ghost instructs and guides me.

This book is a compilation of several smaller books; the task of merging and organizing materials from several sources is an arduous task. I could not have done this without my sister, Joy Ellis Walker, who is also my manager. She edited, typed, retyped, made valuable suggestions for organization and helped me to rework some of the important themes (e.g., 'The Mind Game'). Further, Joy helped me improve my Word Perfect word processing skills which saved me much needed valuable time. My oldest daughter, Jacqueline Butler Williams, also assisted with the editing, particularly verifying the scriptures.

I had friends to support me with much needed assistance, Barbara Ann Baker, Romles Gibbs, Ruth Woods, Joyce Butler Brown, Darlene Ritter and Mother Maggie Jordon, as well as my brothers and sisters, Ralph Nathaniel Ellis, Sr., James Clyde Ellis, Clarence Milton Ellis, Dolores Johnson and Beatrice Walker. My son, Eric and his wife, Cynthia Butler, who are dedicated to the ministry, supported this project also. I appreciate my husband and pastor, Rev. John L. Butler, who continues to be patient, kind, and longsuffering. Craig Williams, a dedicated brilliant young man, is my artist. Boris Collins of LUCN Publishers and Michael Collins and James Moody of Lou-Edna House of Printing gave valuable advice concerning publishing strategies.

I appreciate the prayers and encouragement to merge my small books from Rev. James Lee of South Carolina, Evangelist John Gordon and Evangelist Mary Nunnally of Chicago, Illinois. Michelle Garrison has been a untiring source of encouragement and support.

GLOSSARY

There are a number of terms which are understood differently by different populations, depending on training, church culture, education, and even personal culture. For the purposes of additional clarity, certain terms will be defined in this Glossary.

Baby Saint -- Similar to the natural explanation of an infant, the 'baby saint' is one who is a new Christian who needs compassionate patient spiritual nurturing to grow properly. That is to say, the 'baby saint' will not grow or will grow deformed if not nurtured in the Word of God and prayer.

Born of the 'Spirit' -- The 'spirit of man' is naturally sinful. When a person repents and turns from sin, the Holy Spirit cleanses the old sinful nature and takes up residence in man's spirit.

Christian/saint -- These terms are used interchangeably in this book. The usages of these terms are Bible-based. 'Christian' in this book means, Christ-like. Similarly 'saint' refers to the 'born again' person.

'Die, daily' -- The Bible uses terms like 'mortify your members'(Colossians 3:5) to indicate the responsibility of each 'born again' individual to lay aside and/or stop doing all those things that are contrary to the Word of God. Mortify has two distinct but related meanings; one is 'to discipline one's lust and appetites by self-denial' and the other is 'to cause a body to die'.

'Doorways' -- 'Doorways' are openings for satan to manipulate spiritually and naturally where there are painful experiences of the past which have not been resolved. For example, unforgiveness can be a 'doorway' for resentment, bitterness, hatred, etc.

'Fruits Worthy of Repentance' -- This is the term used in Luke 3:8. As God has opened my understanding, these 'fruits' are humility and contrition, repentance to God, repentance to others, forgiving others and forgiving oneself.

Guilt -- Guilt is a condition of sin. For the saint, guilt is a 'demon'. When you are forgiven, your sins are 'washed away' by God, as though they never happened; your slate is wiped clean. Guilt is the fact of being worthy of punishment for your sins. You cannot be guilty of sin if you are forgiven for sin. The 'feeling of guilt' is a demonic oppression of satan to make you believe you are unworthy of ministry.

The Heart -- Biblically, the term 'heart' refers to the mind, emotions, desire and will as well as the spirit.
There are two Greek works from which 'heart' is translated, 'kardia' and 'pusche'. 'Kardia' also refers to the chief organ of physical life, the heart. By analogy, the metaphor 'heart' deals with center of spiritual life, the location of the individual's desire and true character. 'Psuche' is rendered 'heart' in English but it tends to have a more limited usage, referring more specifically to the soul.

Holiness -- Separation, consecration and dedication to God. Holiness is not absolute perfection but perfect love and obedience to the commandments and will of God.

Holy Spirit/Holy Ghost -- These two terms are used interchangeably. By definition, the Holy Spirit/Holy Ghost is the executive 'agent' of the Godhead operating in the earth through the believers.

'Real Man' -- The 'real man' is not the visible body -- the speech or culture of a person. The 'real man' is the 'spirit of man'.

Slothfulness -- Laziness, sluggishness, failure to exercise any effort, what the old folk called 'sorry' and 'trifling'.

Soul -- Represents man's individuality; the source of man's thinking faculties (the mind and intellect); the source of emotion; the source of the will.

Spirit of Man -- The part of man that never dies and where the Holy Ghost resides (if man meets all prerequisites of repentence and sanctification). The spirit of man is the place of conscience, intuition and the place of communion and communication with God.

'Spirit of Torment' -- The 'spirit of torment' is a demon which can attack the mind, almost around the clock. This 'spirit of torment' is a condition where satan manipulates and oppresses the mind with sinful and negative thoughts while at the same time the person knows that they are saved from their sins. This 'spirit of torment' works well when individuals are not taught that satan's job is to make mental images and sinful desires real. Further, this demon works happily with 'spiritual ignorance'; the lack of understanding that 'resisting the devil' is a daily process.

'Spiritual ignorance' -- 'Spiritual ignorance' is a demon which thrives on the failure of the Christian to understand how efficiently satan functions as the 'prince of this world' and 'the prince of the powers of the air'; he works through subterfuge, conspiracy and deception on the saints, operating in unexpected areas and in unexpected ways.

Will -- Man's purpose, determination and place of self-control.

INTRODUCTION

The legitimate Bible-based heritage of all born again Christians, as 'heirs of God' and 'joint-heirs with Christ', is to be happy, healthy and holy. However, churches everywhere have too many 'saints' or members with unending, on-going, perpetual emotional, mental, physical, financial, social and spiritual crises which are never resolved or ended. **WHAT IS THE PROBLEM??? The fault and failure is not in God.** We are **'CALLED TO BE SAINTS'** (I Corinthians 1:2). If we are **'CALLED TO BE SAINTS'**, we are empowered, endued, and enabled by God to **be saints.**

> *"For the Lord God is sun and shield: the Lord will give grace and glory; no good thing will he withhold from them that walk uprightly (Ps. 84:11).*

Unfortunately, it seems that the norm today is to have a 'form of godliness' (the dancing and shouting, preaching and even most of our praying), but to deny the power of God:[1] There are few being 'saved to the uttermost', few Holy Ghost Baptisms, fewer 'healings' and rare 'deliverances'.

Knowledge has increased and we are ever learning. However, many of us IN THE CHURCH fail to come to the knowledge of **TRUTH** (Jesus)[2], even though Jesus explicitly stated, "I am the Way, the **TRUTH**, and the Light" (John 14:6). Moreover, *"**Be ye holy, for I am Holy**"* (I Peter 1:16) is a **command**, and **absolute order**, not a plea or a request. In

---

[1] **II Timothy 3:5.**

[2] **Daniel 12:4; II Timothy 3:7.**

the Biblical sense 'to be holy' is to be separated, consecrated and dedicated to God and to always be available for God's service.

Notice that the holiness that God expects and requires is not absolute perfection but a perfect love for God (absolute obedience) and the willingness to grow towards perfection. It is mandated to grow in Grace and in the knowledge of our Lord and Saviour, Jesus Christ (II Peter 3:18). Yet the Church, as a whole, has acquired (and continues to pursue) sophisticated knowledge of church administration, church education, church politics, community affairs, public relations, etc., which are worthwhile only if ancillary or subordinate to the Will and Knowledge of God.

Some have already lost or forgotten 'the knowledge of the TRUTH' and are part of the fallen in the 'falling away' (II Thessalonians 2:3). The Word of God indicates, "*My people are destroyed for the lack of knowledge...*" *(Hosea 4:6)*. Consequently, congregations are packed with spiritually fragile and spiritually inconsistent 'saints'. Some of these are 'pillars' in the church and are on the deacon board, the missionary board, the mothers board, in the choir, even in the pulpit. What is the problem? **The fault and failure is not in God.**

> *"But I fear, lest by any means, as the serpent beguiled Eve through his subtilty, so your minds should be corrupted from the simplicity that is in Christ" (II Cor. 11:3).*

The simplicity is, that 'he that comes to Christ and continues to come', according to the conditions set by Christ, will 'in no wise be cast out' (John 6:37). The holiness that God accepts stems from the love we have for God. Jesus said,

> *"If you love me you will obey what I command." (John 14:15)*

> *"And thou shalt love the Lord thy God with **ALL** thy heart,*

*and with **ALL** thy soul, and with **ALL** thy mind, and with **ALL** thy strength: this is the first commandment (Mark 12:30).*

It is apparent that most Christians fall short of the '**ALL**'; there is the insidious weakening of Christian 'experience'. **Haven't you observed** those who have had the 'Seed' (the Word) sown on stony dry ground (Matthew 13:19-20). Their experience is one brief soaring emotional event, where great rejoicing (shouting and dancing) is in evidence. When the music has ceased and the fellowship of the saints removed, the old carnal nature returns. Great energy was expended for a brief period; for a while the Lord was loved with all their strength.

Haven't you also noticed that there are those who readily and repeatedly repent with weeping and sometimes even wailing at the altar, but who never grow in Christ or always backslide? At the seat of their affections and desires -- the heart -- for those brief moments when the Holy Ghost sends conviction, they really desire to live for God. But their heart's desire at other times is for other things.[3]

Haven't you noticed the person who insists that he loves the Lord because he is a lover of his own intellectual ability to study the Word, maybe even preach or teach the Word? This person often goes to Bible School, Seminary, Sunday School and/or Bible Study and may become brilliant and erudite in Biblical studies. This intellectual 'lover of God' is all too often like the self-righteous Pharisee having the letter without the Spirit. Many times these persons believe they are giving God their all.

One of our problems in the church community is that balance is missing. Too many churches 'specialize'; some

---

[3] King Solomon loved the Word and with the wisdom God granted him, ministered the Word. Yet his heart was not perfect with God. His carnal desires, satisfied with Moabite, Ammonite, Edomite, Zidonian, and Hittite women, turned his heart from God (I Kings 11:1-4).

specialize in education--day care centers, Christian academies, etc.; others are "praise" specialists -- bands, choirs, psalmists, praise dancers, etc.; others specialize in fund raising-- teas, cruises, outings, anniversaries, etc.
(Churches need to specialize in developing disciples with the Word of God, prayer ministries and outreach ministries).

In addition, 'slothfulness' is real; churches, leaders and individuals rarely fervently seek God for His vision for the church and community. There is so much education and self-sufficiency in the church community that leaders and laity alike, tend to make and implement plans without consulting God. Presumptuously, after the completion of the plans (God was not consulted about), God is requested to bless those plans.

Individually and collectively, we must return to **THE BASICS** -- seeking God's Will, and living according to God's Will. That can only be accomplished with prayer and Bible based teaching. God has made provision for our perfection in Him through 'balanced' ministries.

> "*And He gave some **APOSTLES**; and some, **PROPHETS**; and some, **EVANGELISTS**; and some **PASTORS** and **TEACHERS**; <u>For the perfecting of the saints, for the work of the ministry, for the edifying of the Body of Christ: Till WE all come in the unity of the faith and of the knowledge of the Son of God, unto a perfect man</u>...*" (Eph. 4:11-14).

Every ministry and gift are in the Body of Christ for the needs of the Body as well as the spread of the Gospel. The ministry of teaching (of necessity) must be included in all the five Gifts mentioned in the above scripture in spite of the fact one Gift is teaching. All too often, the ministry of teaching, basic to kingdom building, is rarely dominant in our churches.

"And He gave some APOSTLES..."
An APOSTLE, in the strictest and classical meaning of the word, was one who was appointed by Christ, who witnessed the resurrection, and who possessed the power of working miracles. Apostles were men who were called and equipped for laying broad and deep foundations of The Church.[4] However in the book of The Acts of the Apostles, there are altogether 18 apostles mentioned, (for example, Barnabus and James the brother of Jesus). Similarly, in these times there are men who have done or are doing apostolic service for God. It should be obvious that apostolic service, that is, laying broad foundations in the church must include **TEACHING**.

"...And some PROPHETS..."
Although the PROPHETS of the Old Testament dealt mainly with 'foretelling', the New Testament prophets of today also speak the Mind of God, but much more 'forthtelling' than Old Testament prophets. Given the nature of the Gift and the Call, the prophetic office will include **TEACHING**.

"...And some EVANGELISTS..."
EVANGELISTS in New Testament times did the work which the church assigns to missionaries today. Phillip, the evangelist, in Acts 8 is pictured in detail as beginning a new work for God in Samaria. Obviously, he had to also teach. However, today's evangelist is really a revivalist, going to churches to revive and restore congregations. Obviously the challenge to be revived and restored is going to come through preaching and **TEACHING**.

"...And some PASTORS and TEACHERS..."
One can consider the ministry of the pastor and teacher as

---

[4] Charles Erdman, <u>The Epistle of Paul to the Ephesians</u> (an exposition) (Baker Book House; Grand Rapids, Mich.) 1988 p 90.

two offices involved in one calling, which is the ministry of the pastor. On the other hand, there are two separate offices assigned to two separate individuals. The critical difference is that the pastor-teacher has the oversight of the local congregation and is involved in continual guidance and instruction. However, the pastor as teacher, as well as the individual who is called and gifted by God as a teacher, must explain the message and mind of God from the completed revelation found in scripture. Therefore, this gift of **TEACHING** goes beyond those that have acquired a skill and have been assigned to teach Bible School or Sunday School.

TEACHING can be with the spoken word. **TEACHING can be** affected through drama. **TEACHING** can be with the written word. If it is Bible based instruction, each approach should edify, mature and bring the saints into the unity of the faith.

The Christian community needs more study tools including those that can be used for group study or self-instruction. This book is for both modalities -- group or individual instruction, for the 'baby' saint as well as the 'mature' saint. This book has been written to fill an increasing need, 'to rightly divide the Word of God'.

Moreover, the pervading persistent theme throughout the book is **personal responsibility for personal growth.** Therefore, the uniqueness of man's individuality and man's ability to choose is explained in the light of the Scriptures in the chapters entitled **'Made in The Image of God', 'A New Creation', 'The Mind Game' and 'Sanctification, A Lifetime Process'**. Having immediate and direct access to the Throne of God and the Power of God is illustrated and illuminated in **'The Weapons Against The Enemy'** and **'How to Know The Will of God For My Life'**.

MADE IN THE IMAGE OF GOD

Consider the awesome uniqueness of man. God is a Spirit; Man has a spirit. God has a will; Man has a will. God has a mind; Man has a mind (soul). God, when he chooses, can manifest angels or Himself in a Body; Man has a body. Just as it is difficult to explain fully the tripartite Godhead, that is, **THE FATHER, THE SON,** and **THE HOLY GHOST,** similarly, it is difficult to fully explain the tripartite nature of man. Sigmund Freud attempted, but his explanations of the 'id'(instinct), 'ego'(the conscious self) and 'superego'(conscience) leaves much to be desired.

Paul, well aware of the tripartite nature of man, wrote to the Thessalonians 'the very God of peace sanctify you (all of you) **WHOLLY**'. Clarifying this further, he wrote, '...*And I pray God your* **WHOLE SPIRIT** *and* **SOUL** *and* **BODY** *be preserved blameless...' (I Thess. 5:23).* Since Paul intentionally separated the three aspects of man, it is necessary for us to explore them.

It is easiest to begin with the **SOUL** because over and over again the Bible refers to men as souls (e.g. Genesis 2:7; 46:27).

SOUL: The soul represent's man's individuality and is the ruling source of our present life.

1. The **soul** is the source of thinking faculties, the mind; intellect (Prov.19:2; Ps.139:14; Prov. 2:10; Prov.3:21,22).
2. The **soul** is the source of emotion (I Samuel 18:1; Song of Solomon 1:7; Ps. 84:2; 86:4; 42:5).
3. The **soul** is the source of the will (Ps.27:12; Job 7:15) The **SOUL** is that part of **SELF-CONSCIOUSNESS.**

SPIRIT: **Man's spirit** (the 'real man') is where God, and the Holy Ghost, will take up His residence, will guide, teach and comfort, if man meets all prerequisites of repentance and sanctification. **Man's spirit**, prior to the fall in the Garden of Eden, was the ruling source in man. When man disobeyed God in the Garden, **his spirit died to God** but remained active in other aspects.

1. **Man's spirit** is 'the place' of conscience which is that part of God in every man (Ps.51:10; Acts 17:16).
2. **Man's spirit** is 'the place' of intuition; that ability to know without knowing how you know. Additionally, intuition is a sensing ability which helps individuals to 'know' while the mind on the other hand, helps individuals to understand (Mark 2:8; Acts 18:5; 20:22).
3. **Man's spirit** is 'the place' of communion and communication with God (John 4:23,24; Romans 1:9).
The **SPIRIT** is that part of man that is **GOD-CONSCIOUS**.

Just a note on the 'spirit of man' to further clarify man's uniqueness...

When the Bible so often speaks of the heart it is generally talking about the 'essence' of man which we tend to call the 'spirit of man' -- man's character and/or man's personality. The Biblical use of the metaphor 'heart' does not refer only to the 'spirit of man' where God desires to dwell. Usually, the term 'heart' is referring to the mind, emotions, will and/or desires as well as the seat of moral and spiritual life which become the control center for what the body does. The 'heart' represents the true character of man which can be controlled and hidden by man for a season; *"For out of the heart come evil thoughts, murder, adultery, sexual immorality, theft, false testimony, slander..."* (Matt. 15:19, NIV).[5]

Notice how the Word of God explains the heart.

> *"But those things which proceed out of the mouth come forth <u>from the heart</u>; and they defile the man. For out of the heart proceed evil thoughts..." (Matthew 15:18,19).*
>
> *"A <u>good man</u> out of the good treasure of the heart bringeth forth good things: and an evil man out of the evil treasure bringeth forth evil things" (Matthew 12:35).*
>
> *"The heart is <u>deceitful **ABOVE** all things,</u> and **desperately wicked**: who can know it? I THE LORD <u>SEARCH THE HEART,</u> I try the reins, even to give every man according to his ways, and according to the fruit of his doings" (Jeremiah 17:9,10).*

Even though God speaks to man through the written Word, the preached Word, music, nature, testimonies and tribulations, man communes with God through man's spirit. That is the reason Jesus said "God is a Spirit and they that worship Him must worship Him in spirit and in truth" (John 4:24). The Lord deals with man spiritually through man's spirit: *"The lamp of the Lord searches the spirit of man; it searches out his inmost being" (Prov. 20:27 NIV).* In other words, you may have mastered scripture, mastered religious ritual (testimonies, messages, choir performances, etc.), but God searches or looks for his presence in your spirit. Paul prayed, *"That He* (JESUS) *would grant you according to the riches of his glory, to be strengthened with might by His Spirit in the inner man (Eph. 3:16).*

---

[5] See APPENDIX II, **The Complexity of the Heart.**

BODY: The place of the five senses, where the lust of the flesh and the lust of the eyes can be stirred to open doorways for satan's control. The simplest definitions are usually best. Therefore suffice it to say that **man is spirit with a soul (mind) which resides in a body.** (See Appendix VII-diagram of the Tripartite Nature of Man, pp. 132, 133.)
MAN HAS CHOICES AND HE MAKES HIS OWN DECISIONS CONCERNING HIS SPIRIT, SOUL AND BODY!!

The greatest and most amazing fact is that because man is made in God's image, God allows man, each man, to make his own choices concerning his spirit, soul and body.

> "Then God said, 'Let us make man in our image, in our likeness, and let them rule over the fish of the sea and the birds of the air, over the livestock, over all the earth, and over all the creatures that move along the ground'" (Genesis 1:26 NIV).

Being made in God's own image means man is spirit or has a spirit, as well as free choice, great reasoning and impressive decision- making power. When man was in the Garden of Eden, his spirit was dominant and in communion with God. **However man had free will and he CHOSE TO DISOBEY GOD.** When man disobeyed God and fell out of fellowship and communion with God, man's 'flesh', that is, his mind and his will became dominant (Genesis 3:3-7).

The Bible does not record how long Adam was in perfect peaceful communication and communion with God. At the time of his disobedience, the reality of God's presence was taken away; all men were brought under the dominion and control of satan. Every man for all time would be born in sin and ready to sin; unbelief, disobedience, rebellion and sinfulness became natural to man.

When Adam disobeyed God and ate of the forbidden fruit, 'the tree of the knowledge of good and evil', he and all mankind died a spiritual death (Genesis 2:17; 3:6). *"Therefore, just as sin entered the world through one man, and death through sin, and in this way death came to all men because all sinned..."(Romans 5:12, NIV).* This meant that man, not only had no relationship and communion with God, but that in his spiritual death, he took on the sin nature of satan. In other words, it became natural for all men to sin.

However man remained the crowning climax of God's creative ability. God gifted man with amazing ability -- to reason and rule. This ability was not destroyed when man fell.

- After Adam fell, man's innate nature became that of **pride, selfishness and rebellion;**
- After Adam fell, man's innate nature became sinful, causing him to become **dissatisfied**, concerning himself with **self-centeredness, self-gratification, and evil.**

Just as Lucifer was not satisfied in heaven and wanted to take over the throne of God, man is never satisfied with his current situation or status. **MAN'S SIN NATURE KEEPS HIM DISSATISFIED.** If he has power, he wants more power; if he has money, he wants more money; if he uses drugs, he needs more drugs. The normal nature of sinful man is self-gratification and self-satisfaction, that is, to be self-serving.

The innate nature of man's character became PRIDE, SELFISHNESS, and REBELLION. Notice, for example, how all infants demand immediate attention by crying loud and long. As the child develops and is undisciplined, the next step will be tantrums. *"Even from birth the wicked go astray; from the womb, they are wayward and speak lies"* (Psalms 58:3, NIV). This behavior will worsen until the child becomes a dangerous completely self-centered adult. As social beings, needing to live among and with others, we learn, of necessity, to give and take.

Our normal nature is to be selfish and evil. In other words, **WE ARE ALL** 'shaped in iniquity'; occurring at the moment of conception."*Surely I was sinful at birth, sinful from the time my mother conceived me...*" *(Psalms 51:5, NIV).*

Man, even though he has been given **a will, must be taught self-control because he controls his destiny** by the decisions he makes all the balance of his days. It is therefore important to understand the concept of man's will if we are to understand the nature of freedom (being saved from sin) or bondage (enslaved in sin and controlled by satan).

Will denotes:
a) strong purpose, intentions and determination;
b) the power of self-direction or self-control.

The concept of the **will** also suggests the end result of a wish, desire or longing. **The operation of the will, then, encompasses also the emotions, and the mind.** You will observe something, think about it, desire (want) it and then make a decision (using your will) to obtain it. Furthermore, no person can violate your will unless you are an imbecile in the truest sense of the word, or 'demon possessed'[6]. **Satan can't violate your will and GOD WON'T.**
Notice how often the Bible uses the word 'let' (referring to your will) which really means that it is each individual's choice **'to allow'** or **'not to allow'**.

"*LET US not be desirous of vain glory...*" *(Gal.5:26).*

"*...LET US cleanse ourselves from all filthiness of the flesh and spirit...*" *(II Cor. 7:1).*

---

[6] If any person is demon possessed, he/she, more than likely, made some decisions that opened 'doorways' to satan's complete control.

"**LET** no corrupt communication proceed out of your mouth..." (Eph. 4:29).

"**LET** all bitterness, and wrath, and anger, and clamor, and evil speaking, be put away from you..." (Eph. 4:31).

"**LET** no man deceive you with vain words..." (Eph 5:6).

"But fornication, and all uncleanness, or covetousness, **LET** it not be <u>once</u> named among you..." (Eph. 5:3).

"**LET** this mind be in you, which was also in Christ Jesus" (Phil. 2:5).

"**LET** your moderation be known unto all men..." (Phil. 4:5).

"**LET** the peace of God rule in your hearts..." (Col.3:15).

In essence, man determines directions and choices by the operation of his **will** all of his life. Consequently man's creativity and genius, controlled by his sin nature, have brought man into such a phenomenal age of technology, science and perversion, that the social, moral and economic fabric of this country, and the world is almost out of control: genetic engineering; cloning; test tube babies; the international but growing drug trade; male, female and child prostitution; the growing power of the military industrial interest groups, etc.

"When I consider your heavens and the work of the your fingers, the moon and the stars, which you have set in place, what is man that you are mindful of him, the son of man that you care for him? You made him a little lower than the heavenly beings and crowned him with glory and honor. You made him RULER OVER THE WORKS OF YOUR HANDS; you put everything under *his feet: all flocks and herds, and the beasts of the field, the birds of the air, and the fish of the sea, all that swim the paths of the seas" (Ps. 8:3-8 NIV).*

Ultimately, it is the fact that man is made in **THE IMAGE OF GOD** (that innate ability to choose decisively), that determines his/her freedom. Every individual decides who he/she associates with, how he/she talks, walks, dresses, eats, prays, reads, etc. Man has a spirit which God gave him. But it is **his will** that he must use to liberate himself from satan's enslavement by agreeing with **God's will**.

Your body or your soul (mind) or your spirit can (and will) come under satanic attack. When Jesus fasted in the wilderness (Matt.4), did not satan attack his mind by suggesting that he, satan, could give him the whole world? Was not his body under attack during passion week prior to and including the crucifixion. In no instance did Jesus yield.

Liberty is a personal choice, but it takes work. Liberty has everything to do with knowing who you are and making positive choices. **Choosing to do anything that an individual wants is license. License disregards others and the consequences of one's actions. God is consummately fair, he allows each person to choose, it can be LIBERTY, LICENSE or SOMETHING IN BETWEEN.**

We can discipline ourselves to be like the psalmist:

*"I WILL sing of your love and justice: O Lord,
I WILL be careful to lead a blameless life -- when will you come to me?
I WILL walk in my house with a blameless heart.
I WILL set before my eyes no vile thing. The faithless men I hate: they WILL NOT cling to me.
Men of perverse heart shall be far from me:
I WILL have nothing to do with evil"
(Ps. 101:1-4, NIV).*

A NEW CREATION

*"Therefore, if any man be **IN CHRIST**, he is a **NEW CREATURE**: old things are passed away; behold all things are become new (II Cor. 5:17).*

When Jesus told Nicodemus that he had to be born again (John 3:3), he wanted Nicodemus to know that 'the real man', (man's spirit), had to be recreated by the Holy Spirit. **Man's spirit, shaped in iniquity, is subject to the power of satan because he is of the 'seed of satan'. Therefore, sinful man, in order to come into God's presence for fellowship, must have a RECREATED SPIRIT.**

All men are dead in their trespasses and sins until they hear the Word, repent, and turn their lives over to Jesus. In other words, **the real man (the spirit) must be 'born again' -- born of the Spirit of God** (John 3:8). **Being born of the 'Spirit of God' means that God cleanses the sinful nature with His Spirit.**

The mystery is, that by the act of faith in the Word (an act of the will) man repents and says **YES, LORD**; the Holy spirit enters and dispossesses the **'old man' (man's sinful nature)** by cleansing **man's spirit with the Blood of Jesus. This is 'being born again'.**

When we confess Christ with our mouth and believe with our hearts (Romans 10:9,10), we are giving the 'hidden man of the heart' over to the work of Calvary. Indeed, man must supply the will and the intellect to bring his soul and spirit into agreement with the Word of God. The Spirit of God then has the freedom to cleanse and recreate the old sinful nature (**man's spirit**) and give man a 'new mind'. If any man, woman, boy or girl is <u>in Christ</u>, that person is a member of the **Body of Christ,** a **joint heir with Christ**, a **child of God;** s/he obviously has to be a new creature.

The **new creature**, the **'born again'** person has a **newly recreated spirit and a new mind.** A new body? -- **NO.** First, understand that the **real man is not the physical body**,-- the looks, the innate talents, or even the intellectual capabilities but the **'spirit of man'**, what Peter *calls the "hidden man of the heart"*[7] and Paul, the *"inward man"*. [8]

Remember, after the body or 'fleshly tabernacle is dissolved' in physical death, **man's spirit can** live forever. In order for this to be possible, Jesus had to suffer the wrath of God for us and die a horrible sinful death.

> *"Yet it pleased the Lord to bruise him; he hath put him to grief: when thou shalt make his soul an offering for sin... He shall see of the travail of his soul and shall be satisfied..." (Isaiah 53:10,11; cf Romans 5:18).*

The plan of redemption was completed when "...*Christ was raised up from the dead BY THE GLORY OF THE FATHER..." (Romans 6:4).* This means simply, that as soon as the individual repents and accepts by faith[9] the penalty paid by Jesus, he or she is justified or saved. *"Therefore being justified by faith, we have peace with God through our Lord Jesus Christ" (Romans 5:1).*

The greatest miracle and spiritual phenomena is *"But as many as received Him, to them gave He power to become the sons of God" (John 1:12).* The receiving of the sonship of

---

[7] **II Corinthians 4:16.**

[8] **I Peter 3:4**

[9] **Faith is not just an intellectual agreement with something; it also involves acting on what the individual believes.**

God, the NEW BIRTH, (man's **CREATION EXPERIENCE**) empowers man to work for God.

Understanding how to be saved and knowing what it means to be saved, is not the same as being saved. Therefore, the Christian must always be willing to look 'inward' and reevaluate his/her relationship with God and man. Being 'born again' involves more than a verbal confession of sin. To be sure we understand **'repentance' or 'the new creation'**, review what God considers **'FRUITS WORTHY OF REPENTANCE'**.

HAVE YOU BROUGHT 'FRUITS WORTHY OF REPENTANCE'? Realize that if godly sorrow worketh repentance, **'fruits worthy of repentance' are those 'fruits' which God ACCEPTS which are:**

1. **A contrite and humble spirit.**
2. **The willingness to repent to God.**
3. **The willingness to repent to others.**
4. **The willingness to forgive others.**
5. **The willingness to forgive yourself.**

We claim to have accepted Christ and we state we are new creatures in Him (II Corinthians 5:17). However, we need to look 'inward' and do as the 'Angel of the Church at Ephesus' told the saints at Ephesus:

> "REMEMBER *therefore from whence thou art fallen*, and **REPENT**, *and do the first works; or else I will come unto thee QUICKLY, and will remove thy candlestick out of his place, except thou repent*" (Rev. 2:5).

The beginning of our first works was repentance. John, the Baptist, ordered *'bring fruits worthy of repentance'* (Luke 3:8; cf Matthew 3:8). In the model prayer, **THE LORD'S PRAYER**, which Jesus taught to those who followed Him, *'forgive us our sins'* was emphasized (Luke 11:4). We are not perfect because we are still engaged in spiritual warfare, the carnal versus the spiritual. We are not sinners, but we are not sinless. Before indignation and shock sets in, consider your **sins of omission**.[10] Did not James write: *"Therefore to him that knoweth to do good, and doeth it not, to him it is sin" (James 4:17).* Therefore, **daily** we must bring forth fruits worthy of repentance.

THE WORTHY FRUITS

1. **A Contrite and Humble Spirit.**

God cannot stand and will not tolerate the spirit or even the appearance of pride (Proverbs 6:16,17; 16:18). The basis for the first sin and the greatest rebellion of all eternity was the pride of Lucifer (Isaiah 14:12; Ezekiel 28:12-19). He had what he considered reasons to be proud -- his beauty, his brilliance, his political and military 'clout'. However, since God had granted him this favor, his pride was foul. Likewise, whatever we are or have become, it is because God has allowed this to be so. Pride, gives self the credit and excludes God.

On the other hand, *"The Lord is nigh unto them that are of a broken heart; and saveth such as be of a contrite spirit" (Psalm 34:18).* Contrite, according to Webster's Dictionary, means grieving and penitent for sin and shortcomings. Notice then, the Lord is kept distant from you if your 'heart' is proud and hardened.

"The sacrifices of God are a broken spirit: a broken and contrite heart, O God, thou will not despise (Ps. 51:17).

---

[10] For example: (1) failure to call that missing member when he comes to your mind ; or (2) failure to obey specific instructions from your pastor or leader when it is in your power to do so.

When the individual finally comprehends and accepts the wonder of God's Love and the awesomeness of Christ's sacrificial death for his/her offensive sins, brokenness and contrition is the normal response. Or, if you have already been saved and then sinned again, your heart and spirit are broken because you have crucified or opened Jesus' wounds afresh (Heb. 6:6). It is easy to humble oneself under the **MIGHTY HAND OF GOD.** Consider the sovereignty of God; **MAJESTY, DOMINION, GLORY AND POWER belongs to HIM.** Yet, as **GREAT** as He is, He has accepted us as sons and daughters. **Awesome thought!!!**

Riches, education, power and popularity do not count with God. Until we humble ourselves God cannot dwell with us or minister to us.

"For thus saith the high and lofty One that inhabiteth eternity, whose name is Holy; I dwell in the high and holy place with him also that is of a contrite and humble spirit, to revive the spirit of the humble, and to revive the heart of the contrite ones" (Is. 57:15).

If you are having trouble renouncing that (demon) "spirit of pride", do as David did; he humbled his soul with fasting (Psalms 35:13). Go on a couple of three or seven day fasts; the weakness of your flesh will assure you that you are little more than nothing.

2. **The Willingness to Repent to God.**
When the scripture orders us to **bring forth fruits 'worthy of repentance'** (Luke 3:8; Matthew 3:8), **the word repentance infers a real change of mind and attitude towards sin and its causes, not merely its consequences.**
Many times individuals are sorry about a sin but are not willing to change. **The repentance that God accepts is based on total surrender.** Individuals must see themselves filthy and nasty and totally unfit for God's holiness because "...*we*

are *ALL as an unclean thing, and all our righteousness are as FILTHY RAGS..."(Isaiah 64:6).*

> *"Repent ye therefore, and be converted that your sins may be blotted out, when the times of refreshing shall come from the presence of the Lord" (Acts 3:19).*

REMEMBER, TRUE REPENTANCE BRINGS TRUE DELIVERANCE. Without repentance and turning from all sin, you cannot have the **Spirit of God abiding in your spirit..**

3. **The Willingness to Repent to Others**

> *"Therefore if thou bring thy gift to the altar, and there rememberest that thy brother hath ought against thee: leave there thy gift before the altar, and go thy way; first be reconciled to thy brother, and then come and offer thy gift" (Matthew 5:23,24).*

You cannot progress in God over that wounded brother or sister. It seems that one of the most difficult things is for one person to go to another and say, "*I am sorry, I was wrong*". However, God cannot accept you or your gifts (your prayers, praises or your church work) until **YOU REPENT AND MAKE PEACE** with your brother and sister.

4. **The Willingness to Forgive**
There are many among us in the church who love the Lord, who are not yet spiritually whole or emotionally healed. Some have had childhoods or marriages during which they were abused physically, psychologically, sexually and/or emotionally. Many males and females, adults and children, have been **raped and/or have been the victims of incestuous**

relationships.[11] Others have been **exploited on the job, or by relatives, and ignored and/or mistreated in the church.** Most times these persons have been heinously and unfairly treated usually through no fault of their own. **No person is responsible for the actions of others, but <u>God holds us responsible for our actions and reactions</u>.**

GOD CANNOT HEAL YOUR HURTS NOR FORGIVE YOUR SINS UNTIL <u>YOU FORGIVE</u>

"And when ye stand praying, forgive, if ye have ought against any: that your Father also which is in heaven may forgive you your trespasses (Mark 11:25, 26; cf Matthew 6:14,15).

The Lord, in the book of Hebrews, explicitly instructed:

"Follow peace with all men, and holiness, without which no man shall see the Lord: looking diligently less ANY MAN fail of the Grace of God; lest any root of bitterness springing up trouble you, and thereby many be defiled (Hebrews 12:14).

Grace is the unmerited favor of God -- favor we do not deserve and cannot earn. There is nothing we can do to make us worthy of Christ's death and suffering. He willingly took each individual's sins upon himself and then forgives

---

[11] In the nineties, the incidence and prevalence of sexual abuse of every type is increasing rapidly. In some areas, 1 in 3 women and 1 in seven males have been sexually abused.

each person who repents of those sins that he has already died for (Romans 5:8).

When we refuse to forgive, we fail the Grace of God. You may feel the perpetrator or violator of your rights or your person is not worth forgiving and does not deserve forgiveness. NOT ONE OF US DESERVES FORGIVENESS; it is given freely even though it is unmerited. When you fail God by not forgiving, you place yourself in satan's territory.

Satan never stops!!! **The 'unforgiving spirit' gives way to the 'spirit' or 'root of bitterness'.** Think of how graphic the metaphor **'root'** is. A **root** is hidden, and unobservable but it has life in a dark place. The **root** grows and spreads before it surfaces showing itself. **If you do not forgive, bitterness will defile you, and because, it has sprung up, it will be observable to others as well.**

Has it occurred to you that the person whom you did not forgive, or feel that you are unable to forgive, is still controlling you through your emotions? That person may be in ALASKA, ALABAMA, AUSTRALIA, or even in the grave.

THINK ABOUT IT !!!

This person or persons who hurt, mistreated or violated you, continues to manipulate you because you are holding the hurts and wounds. Your personality, your soul, and even your countenance are defiled because of past deeds committed **AGAINST** you for which <u>you have not forgiven</u>.

EXAMPLE # 1

The Lord blessed me to minister to a friend, whose husband had abandoned her and her children, married again and became a successful preacher in a church of a different denomination. Not only had he moved her thousands of miles from her home state and family, but he also sexually violated one of their daughters. The daughter has been an emotional and

mental wreck since, exhibiting deviant behavior ranging from drug abuse and prostitution to abandonment of her illegitimate children.

Consequently, the wife hated her husband with intense unrelenting hatred. She claimed salvation and was active in her church, but she verbally stated she could not give up her hatred. Only when the Lord gave me a Word of Wisdom to show her that this man was still controlling her through her hatred, and sending her to hell as well, was she able to renounce and dispossess this 'spirit of hatred', forgive her former husband and THEN BE HEALED.

EXAMPLE # 2

Another friend, a deacon, for many years in his church, who was faithful with the stewardship of his finances, and who ministered in a public institution for homeless men, was driven with restlessness, impatience, anger, fear, hostility, inferiority, etc. His wife asked me to come by to see him. After talking to him and writing the list of "demon spirits" that seemed to be oppressing him, I instructed him to rebuke and renounce all of them in the Name of Jesus. When we finished praying, I asked him how did he feel. His reply was, "I feel better but I don't believe I will make the rapture". I told him I would return that night; I had to return to my place of employment.

I returned with my Co-Worker, Chaplain Barbara Williams, Sr. We went over the list of 13 different demon spirits oppressing him, telling him to renounce them and plead the Blood of Jesus against each one of them. Then, while we were praying, the Lord gave a Word of Knowledge, 'hatred for his son-in-law'. He was told to forgive his son-in-law and renounce that demon of hatred. Satan bound his mouth, contorted his face and even changed his voice. 'Hatred' was the 'ruling spirit' which gave access to all the other 'spirits' mentioned above. Since this was the 'ruling spirit', satan did not want to give up that easily. But with prayer and the power of the Holy Ghost, this 'spirit' was bound and cast out. He renounced hatred (forever) in the Name of Jesus.

As it turned out, the son-in-law had beaten, and abused his only daughter more than once. He had previously forgiven him and gave him an excellent job in his business. After the last episode during which the son-in-law not only stabbed his daughter, but also threatened to kill him and blow up his entire business. The 'rage', 'resentment', 'anger' and 'hatred' began to torment him so much that he could not sleep nights nor relax during the day. Further, he was irritable, impatient and short tempered with his wife whom he loved. He was not free to renounce and dispossess the demons tormenting him until he forgave.

He forgive his son-in-law, then asked the Lord to forgive him, and also to cover his family and possessions with the Blood of Jesus. PEACE REIGNED.

Remember, if you do not forgive, you have opened 'doorways' and **HAVE GIVEN** satan an opening to oppress you with other 'unclean spirits' that war against the soul and emotions.

An 'unforgiving spirit' leads to spirits of 'bitterness', 'loneliness', 'self-pity', 'depression', 'rejection', 'inferiority', 'resentment', 'anger', 'rage', 'wrath', 'hatred', etc., etc., etc.

To be free; FORGIVE

To remain free; FORGIVE

To be attack proof; FORGIVE

To grow in God; FORGIVE

5. **The Willingness to Forgive Yourself**
When you have not forgiven yourself, you suffer with guilt, low self-esteem, insecurity and the inability to be free of the past. Many who have accepted the Lord and are living free from sin, have histories that plague their thoughts and make these persons miserable.

FORGIVE YOURSELF!

Don't let the tyranny of your past burden you; **JESUS HAS 'WIPED' YOUR SLATE CLEAN'.**

"As far as the east is from the west, so far hath he removed our transgressions from us" (Psalms 103:12).

"For I will be merciful to their unrighteousness, and their sins and their iniquities will I remember no more" (Hebrews 8:12).

"...I will put my laws into their hearts, and in their minds will I write them. And their sins and iniquities will I remember no more" (Hebrews 10:16,17).

Once you have repented and received Jesus, you are a new creature (II Corinthians 5:17) because the precious blood has washed away **ALL** your sins. If your past comes up, only **YOU, SATAN, AND SOMEONE SATAN IS USING** remembers it, **GOD DOESN'T**. Recognize the fact that Satan will use the past to hinder the Spirit of God working through you. For example, God will urge you to witness or pray for someone. Satan will bring a feeling of unworthiness by resurrecting some thoughts of your past sinful life to stop you.

If you function based on your feelings you are surrendering yourself to demonic intimidation and manipulation. Victory, peace and power is not based on feelings, but on the fact of your surrender and obedience to The Word of God.

> "There is therefore now NO CONDEMNATION to them which are in Christ Jesus, who WALK NOT AFTER THE FLESH, but after the Spirit. For the law of the Spirit of Life in Christ Jesus HATH MADE ME FREE from the law of sin and death" (Romans 8:1,2).

WHATEVER HAS HAPPENED, HAPPENED!!!
THE PAST IS OVER!!!

You are completely free and God does not consider anything that happened before your 'new birth'. "You are free and he who the Son has set free is free indeed" (John 8:36). You are free to work for God.

Each one of us is responsible for bringing 'fruits worthy of repentance', or in other words, **fruits which God accepts.** They are:

1. A **CONTRITE** and **HUMBLE** spirit.

2. The **WILLINGNESS TO REPENT** to God.

3. The **WILLINGNESS TO REPENT** to others.

4. The **WILLINGNESS TO FORGIVE** others.

5. The **WILLINGNESS TO FORGIVE** yourself.

SELF-EXAMINATION #1
A NEW CREATION

1. Do you regularly humble yourself to God by regularly fasting and praying, at least twice a week?

2. Do you humble yourself in small things by giving up that special seat to another member or visitor in your church?

3. Are you ready and willing to say, "*I am sorry, I was wrong*" to those you may have wronged or hurt only a little?

4. Have you really forgiven that person who hurt you and violated your trust?

5. Can you earnestly pray for the soul of the person who offended you?

6. Do you pity yourself frequently?

7. Are you aching with loneliness?

8. Do you feel resentment over other's blessings and progress?

9. Are you plagued by feelings of inferiority?

10. Do you constantly try to relive the past by wishing you had not done a particular thing?

Conscious Mind

Subconscious Mind

UnConscious Mind

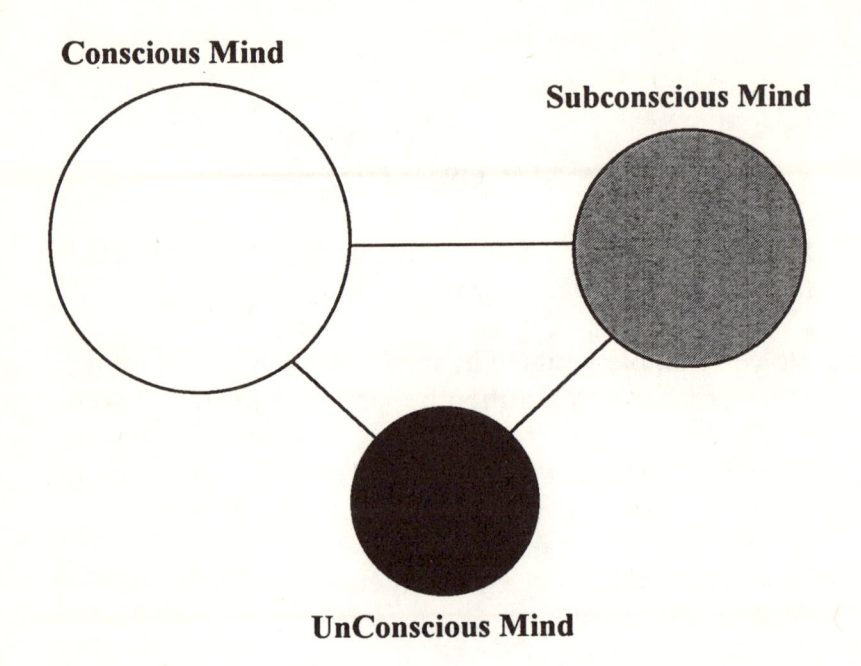

A Diagram of the different levels of consciousness.

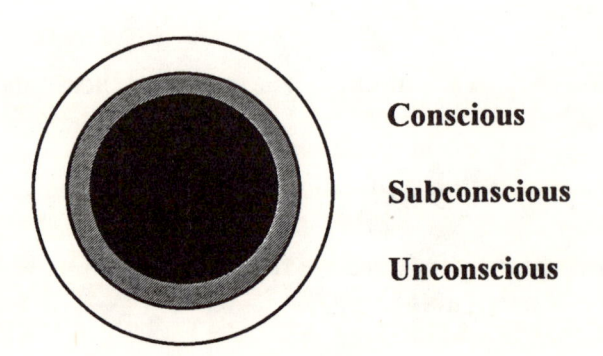

Conscious

Subconscious

Unconscious

A Diagram of the interrelatedness of the conscious, subconscious and unconscious mind.

THE MIND GAME

THE BATTLE IS IN THE MIND!!!

- **The Battle is in the Mind** because the mind controls the desire of man's spirit.

- **The Battle is in the Mind** because it is with the mind the Word of God is heard and rejected or received.

What is the Mind?

As discussed in Chapter 2 ('Made in the Image of God'), the mind is that element of the soul that represents man's individuality -- his emotions, thinking faculties, memory, will and reasoning ability.

Understand the magnificent sophistication of the mind; **conscious, subconscious and unconscious mind.** Even as you are reading your **conscious mind** is analyzing, absorbing, and/or rejecting what you are reading. Much of what you are reading is stored in your **subconscious mind** and can quite readily be recalled.

On the other hand, the **unconscious mind** is the place where memories of the distant past are stored, particularly the painful memories. Moreover, **painful recent experiences** may be stored in the **unconscious mind.**

The **unconscious mind** (as described in this book) is most appropriately described as the place of mental activity and past experiences that the **conscious mind** is totally unaware of. First of all, **ALL THAT IS STORED IN THE UNCONSCIOUS MIND CAN AFFECT CURRENT REALITY.** This is a critical point.

(I have observed individuals functioning under a burden of low self-esteem, inadequacies, etc. even though they have been freed from sin and the past. This is satan's method of manipulating the believer with those feelings related to past events and/or experiences which have been buried in the unconscious -- which they do not remember.) **But know that when you become saved, the slate is wiped clean! You are now a new creation, even though experiences of THE PAST (which are stored in your unconscious mind) are not erased from your mind!**

SATAN CANNOT READ YOUR MIND!

Nevertheless, satan, 'full of wisdom' (Ezekiel 28:12), knows all you have done and every demonic force you were exposed to. Further, much of your past you do not remember (which as we mentioned above is stored in your unconscious mind), but satan does.

Satan's demons were there when such negative experiences occurred, such as:
- In childhood you were disciplined more than loved;
- and/or if you were criticized more than encouraged;
- and/or if you were physically, sexually and psychologically abused;
- and/or if you physically and sexually abused someone;
- and/or if you even murdered someone or committed some other heinous act.

In addition, satan can spiritually limit, intimidate and destroy you by working in those areas of your life that you are weak in - - **but only if you allow him.**

Unfortunately for most of us, we fail to realize that **satan will manipulate us by feelings related to the past for which we have been forgiven and for which we have repented.**

After you have been set free from sin and bondage, you may feel miserable at times, **because satan wants you to operate on your feelings. GUILT, LOW SELF-ESTEEM, REJECTION, FEAR, UNWORTHINESS, RAGE, ANGER,** etc., are all emotions and feelings which demon spirits will oppress a born again individual with time and time again.

Satan will send the same demon spirit that had you

miserable and in bondage, to torment you. You will feel tormented if you do not understand that he is oppressing you. Be Aware That:

1. **Satan works in the area of your vulnerability.** e.g., If you have been delivered from a 'lust' demon, he will keep sending that lust demon around you to make you feel that he is still in you.
2. **Satan will accompany these feelings with 'lying spirits'** telling you that you can not be saved, because you would not be going through (or feeling) what you are going through. Remember, 'demon spirits' normally do not work alone. Further, when you accept the Lord the old 'spirit'(s) seek reinforcements (Matthew 12:44).
3. Once satan starts challenging you spiritually, **and you do not use the Word of God, The Blood of Jesus, and The Name of Jesus against him**, you will also be suffering with a **'spirit of torment'**.
4. A **'spirit of torment'** for the saint is when your **mind (soul)** is troubled because of what you are experiencing in your **mind (thoughts and dreams)** and in your **flesh (desires and emotions)**. At the same time you know you love God and have repented and turned from all sin. You've surrendered unto God, but you are under attack by satan and his demons and you think that this is you.

As discussed earlier, when you repented, your slate was wiped clean by God as though these things never happened. Nevertheless, satan and his demons were there when these negative experiences occurred and are yet well aware of the feelings and emotions you felt -- **THE GUILT, LOW SELF-ESTEEM, REJECTION, FEAR, UNWORTHINESS, RAGE, ANGER,** etc.

SATAN CANNOT READ YOUR MIND, BUT WAS THERE WHEN ALL THE NEGATIVE EXPERIENCES OCCURRED, SO HE <u>ATTACKS THE MIND</u>!

"Baby" saints are uniquely vulnerable to these kinds of attacks on the mind. The "baby" saint who knows he/she has made a total commitment to live for Jesus will be attacked by a **'spirit of torment'**.

A **'spirit of torment'** is mental anguish that is a combination of fear of failure and uncertainty about one's salvation, when in fact, the individual knows he/she has given her heart to the Lord. Actually, the person under attack by the **'spirit of torment'** feels divided because satan is talking to the mind, while the 'spiritual man' is crying out to God.

The person, who is under attack by a **'spirit of torment'**, may be bombarded by 'old' or even 'new' desires, feelings and thoughts. The saint becomes so embarrassed, not realizing that these are satanic spirits oppressing him/her, that he/she will be too ashamed to seek prayer and counseling. Then satan will send **'lying spirits'** to talk to the saint with the voice of their own mind and tell him/her that she cannot possibly be saved, feeling or thinking like this. **'Spiritual ignorance'** is a demonic device that can destroy innocent Christians and this works with the **'spirit of torment'**.

The Case of the Ex-Addict

I was in revival in a church where a young man was crying and struggling and praying. After praying with him for a few moments, the Lord gave me a 'Word of Knowledge' to let him know that God had delivered him from drugs and that he was indeed free. Secondly, that being exposed to marijuana contact inhalation on his job, resurrecting old carnal desires in his flesh, was not sin. The Lord further instructed me to tell him temptation was not sin and that satan was working in the area of his lack of understanding and weakness. The Lord gave me a Word of Wisdom

to tell him how to 'cover himself with the Blood of Jesus' every day; also to talk back to satan every time he sent any desire or thought that was not of God.

IT IS SATAN'S JOB AND MISSION TO MAKE THE BELIEVER FEEL UNWORTHY, GUILTY AND USELESS!

The device that satan uses is to bring so much shame and guilt to the mind of an innocent saint that he/she will FEEL unworthy and unsaved. Then satan convinces the individual that he/she may as well backslide.[12]

To be certain that the person **remains bound and ineffective, satan will add to the GUILT of the feelings, the GUILT of failure, especially if he knows he cannot make the saint backslide.**

Whenever you feel this way, **and function based on your feelings**, satan has gotten a victory over your life. Think of how often God has given you a vision of something to do in your ministry or church. When satan finished manipulating you, first through your feelings, and then through your mind, you failed to do that which God had given you to do. Disobedience for any reason is sin (James 4:17).

Furthermore, satan can attack the mind when **'flashbacks'** of the painful past begin to surface in the conscious mind and/or in dreams. When these **'flashbacks'** occur, the 'presence' or 'feelings' of the experiences of the past also surface. **Immediately, because you are feeling what you are remembering, 'the guilt of sin' (a demon spirit) also presents himself.** Some experiences are so horrible, that even if you are innocent, the 'guilt' is yet very real. Take for example, a female child who has been the victim of incest. Whenever that experience presents itself in a **'flashback'**, demons of

---

[12] Talking back to satan can be a simple as saying, NO, IN THE NAME OF JESUS, NO!! Satan and his demon spirits sent to torment you will know what this means.

'GUILT', 'UNWORTHINESS', 'SHAME', 'LOW SELF-ESTEEM' present themselves.

If your past was plagued with multiple experiences of abuse and misery which were locked up in the unconscious mind, God may allow the healing process to be gradual. I ministered to a woman over a period of six years during which God allowed only one experience at a time to surface. These events were so traumatic, satan would have destroyed her mind completely if they had surfaced all at once.

This is a summary of the trauma:
1. Her mother's boy friend sexually assaulted her at the age of seven. Believing she was lying, her mother slapped and punished her, when she reported the abuse to her mother.
2. From the age of 9 to 16, three of her older brothers regularly sexually assaulted her. This stopped when she accepted the Lord.
3. At 17 on her first job, she was raped, sodomized and physically misused in numerous horrible ways. She made it home but was not talking. Because she was in a state of catatonia[13], she was admitted to an institution for a year.
4. During that year while catatonic and not talking, the men on staff regularly sexually assaulted her as well as the lesbians. She gradually improved and was released but remained in a Christian home (away from her family) until she recovered.
5. She eventually married a man who her mother and her pastor begged her not to marry. Hungering for love, she married him anyhow and became a **'DOORMAT'**. This man beat her physically and psychologically tormented her by calling her stupid and ignorant for 12 years. She took these offenses until he left.

---

[13] **Catatonia is a trance-like state; the person does not speak.**

At the time I came in contact with her none of the above was remembered except the experiences in her marriage. Even though she was reclaimed, her personality was remorseful, and was evidencing extreme low self-esteem. She had to be ministered to constantly.

Notice that at each deliverance session when a 'flash back' was occurring, the experience was replayed in her mind and body[14]**; she felt the actual pain of the abuse.** After a session in which the events listed in the above Item 4 were remembered, she went into a state of depression. The Lord showed me a 'suicide spirit'. I went to her home and told her I saw her with a hand full of pills about to take them. She admitted that the previous evening she was preparing to take a bottle full of pills, but the Lord stopped her. She decided she could not take any more 'flashbacks' because they were too painful. God gave me the wisdom to explain to her that:

1. **She was never alone when she had a 'flashback';**
2. **The Holy Ghost was always there to minister when she had a 'flashback';**
3. **The 'flashbacks' were necessary in order to deal with the emotions and feelings of inferiority and unworthiness that were always lingering.**

Fortunately, the 'flashbacks' ended. Her personality and ministry then began to change. She was able to recognized abused women and minister to them.

---

[14] After the writer discussed with a gynecologist the physical affects of 'demons' of sexual abuse, the gynecologist indicated that her medical experience verifies this. While Chief resident at a renown Metropolitan area hospital and an attending physician at St. Luke's Hospital in Manhattan, she said she has had many clinic patients presenting with vaginal pain. She rarely found any pathology. But for those who were willingly to discuss social history, many admitted being victims of sexual abuse.

NOTE:
Lest there appears to be some confusing issues in the discussion, we do affirm that when you are saved you are completely saved. Your mind, intentions and desires are new, and 'swept clean' of satan's contamination. Experiences, however, are not erased from your memory. The protective device, when experiences are too traumatic, is to 'block it' out of the conscious memory. If all of the negative experiences were recalled at the same time, a 'nervous breakdown' might occur.

The following example reveals how, if many previous horrible experiences surface all at one time, the results will be woeful:

Example

Evangelist G, who is a witch that is masquerading as an evangelist, was running a revival in one Holiness church. Every person she physically touched with her hands fell out. She gave what was perceived as prophetic words. (Satan has demons working all the time and can feed facts about an individual's past history or present needs, to any of his servants or witches in order to deceive the people of God). The congregation was impressed and became vulnerable to this damnable ministry. One young woman, a minister's wife, had a mental breakdown and had to be hospitalized after Evangelist G. prayed for her. Immediately after receiving prayer from this witch, many horrible experiences surfaced from her unconscious mind, <u>all at one time</u>. Her memory was so confused that the episodes of what occurred was not very clear, nor were the persons responsible.

After her husband and the saints fasted and prayed, she improved somewhat but not entirely. She has not been able to really look at the past, clearly identify the facts and consequently deal with those occurrences. The

experiences, after prayer by this witch, surfaced as a nightmarish conglomeration of horror.

The key is to recognize that even though you are saved, there are experiences in the past that can affect your freedom in God. Therefore, it is in God's plan for your maturity for you to be able to deal with the painful past. The only way to be healed of emotional, mental, physical and sexual trauma, is to look at events, go through the forgiveness process and then allow our compassionate Lord and Saviour heal the hurt and the pain.

Satan is so sophisticated at these mind games, that the saint can not even afford to spend time thinking about the painful past. If you begin thinking about those experiences, you have opened a 'doorway' for satan to torment the mind and flesh. Immediately **'CLOSE THOSE DOORWAYS'**. (A 'doorway' is any emotion or desire that's not of God that you 'entertain' or dwell on; this gives satan access to your spirit.)

HOW YOU CAN AND MUST CLOSE THOSE 'DOORWAYS'

1. **Repent to God**. Even though you may not have done anything, you must make sure satan realizes that you will give him no grounds to defeat, destroy or hinder you. Even though you are saved, simply tell God you are sorry for all sin related to this event. **This sounds like a paradox or contradictory when you were innocent in the first place, and in the second place that the 'slate of sin' was wiped clean at your initial conversion. All you are doing is letting satan know that you mean to stand in a right relationship with God, even to the extent that you are willing to repent for sins that you did not perpetrate.** Satan knows then you are not open to all the other past, but similar, painful occurrences and he cannot manipulate

your mind with them. Satan also knows that he cannot manipulate you through your emotions by causing you to make irrational and impractical decisions. This way no uncleanness will be able to enter your mind or spirit.

2. **Forgive the offenders**[15]. This closes the door to spirits of 'revenge', 'anger', 'rage', 'hatred', 'unforgiveness', 'murder', etc.
3. **Forgive yourself.** This closes the door to 'guilt' and 'self-condemnation' which impact on your freedom to minister for God.
4. **Praise God and ask God in THE NAME OF JESUS OF NAZARETH to allow the Holy Ghost to take up residence and seal all those areas of the mind where satan wanted to torment.**

Furthermore, **God wants us to be able to remember the past without the pain. God heals the pain of the memories when we forgive; then the doorways are closed to satan.**

Thus, it is imperative that you learn to **RESIST THE DEVIL!!** Satan attacks when your feelings and emotions are most vulnerable because of **'spiritual ignorance'.**

'Spiritual ignorance' is a powerfully deceptive demon which causes the individual to condemn him/herself for the oppressive polluted thoughts that satan sends to their mind. Satan works 24 hours a day. He will send you horrible dreams or even nightmares. He will bring foul, even polluted thoughts and desires to your mind during the day. The major and continuing battle is in THE MIND. If satan can control and manipulate your mind, he can manipulate your emotions and actions. **The one thing a saint cannot do and remain saved, is to honor, listen to, or reason with an evil spirit.**

Satan and his lying oppressive spirits are deliriously happy when you begin to accuse yourself by saying, "why am I

---

[15] The principles of forgiveness are discussed in greater detail in Chapter 3, 'A New Creation'.

thinking this?". Satan's back-up demons will begin to insist with the voice of your own mind that 'you cannot possibly be saved thinking these thoughts.'

*"The weapons of our warfare are not carnal, but mighty through God to the pulling down of strongholds, casting down imaginations... and bringing into captivity **EVERY THOUGHT** to the obedience of Christ (II Cor. 10:4,5).*

Resist the devil and **he will flee. Resisting the devil demands consistency and competence.**

RESISTING THE DEVIL IS:
- • Understanding that you are not saved by feelings, but by faith, obedience and repentance.

- • Understanding that you can not even begin to wonder WHY you are having these experiences. If you are saved, and you do not like what you are feeling, and experiencing, it is probably of the devil.
Simply **rebuke, renounce, bind, dispossess and cast out everything that you feel or fear by saying, 'SATAN, THE LORD REBUKE YOU'**; or say (by naming what you feel), **'Spirit of_____', I bind, rebuke and cast out in the Name of Jesus of Nazareth'.**
Send all the demons back 'to dry places' (after they are 'bound' and 'cast out' from your presence and/or your home).[16]

- • <u>Understanding</u> that as often as Satan and his demons challenge your salvation and your peace, **you must again BIND, REBUKE AND CAST OUT IN THE NAME OF**

---

[16] Matthew 18:18, Luke 11:24.

JESUS! Every day, if necessary.[17]

- - Understanding that you must always ask the Lord to allow his BLOOD to wash you again and cover you continuously. **Pray, Lord, allow your BLOOD TO WASH MY MIND, including MY SUBCONSCIOUS AND MY UNCONSCIOUS MIND, MY WILL, MY DREAMS, MY EMOTIONS, MY DESIRES, MY BODY, MY PERSONALITY free of all satan's spots and attack.**

- - Understanding that there is one Baptism but many Fillings. Ask the Lord to fill you again with His Spirit.

- - Understanding also that satan hates **THE WORD OF GOD**. Therefore, there are certain key scriptures you must memorize and use them when satan starts his attack.

"And they overcame him with the BLOOD OF THE LAMB and the WORD OF THEIR TESTIMONY; and they loved not their lives unto the death (Rev. 12:11).

"Behold I GIVE UNTO YOU POWER *to tread on* SERPENTS *and* SCORPIONS, *and over* ALL THE POWER *of the enemy; and nothing shall by any means hurt you*" (Luke 10:19).

---

[17] Corrie Ten Boom in her book, **TRAMP FOR THE LORD,** described the pain and fear of a young girl who had been 'demon possessed' and then delivered. In the following year, when Corrie Ten Boom returned to the church of this young woman. She was tormented because of the 'demon spirits'. Corrie Ten Boom explained to her that when the sexton stop pulling the cord that rings the bell in the belfry, it will soon stop. But until it stops, the ringing is just an echo. THE POWER BEHIND THE RINGING IS GONE. She instructed her to continue praying and doing all the things that she knew to do and after awhile, the 'demons' would stop oppressing her.

"Ye are of God little children and have overcome them: because greater is he that is in you than he that is in the world" (I John 4:4).

"For Whatsoever is born of God overcometh the world; and this is the victory that overcometh the world, even our faith (I John 5:4).

There are many other scriptures. For example, read Psalms 44:5; Isaiah 54:17; Matthew 18:18. Start memorizing these and other scriptures. **When you quote them aloud, you are strengthened, and satan's power is weakened.** Since he is the 'father of lies' and 'a liar from the beginning', he hates TRUTH (John 8:44). **USE THE WORD OF GOD DAILY.**

The mind controls the desire of man's spirit. In other words, satan will keep the mind occupied with all kinds of **self-centeredness like self-pity, inferiority, depression, pride, greed,** in order to prevent you from seeking and yielding to the perfect Will of God. That's why the scripture instructs:

"Finally, brethren, whatsoever things are true, whatsoever things are honest, whatsoever things are just, whatsoever things are pure, whatsoever things are lovely, whatsoever things are of good report; if there be any virtue, and if there be any praise, **think on these things**" *(Phil. 4:8).*

There are many born again persons who do not 'feel' free but are free indeed. These persons need to pray like the psalmist:

"Search me, O God, and know my heart: try me, and know my thoughts: And see if there be any wicked way in me, and lead me in the way everlasting" (Psalm 139:23,24).

At the other end of the spectrum are the **deceptions** that satan sends to those who believe they can not be deceived.; Believing that you cannot be deceived is a satanic **deception**.

Satan can and does work believable 'lying wonders'. Satan does run healing campaigns and miracle working campaigns that look and sound like the Holy Ghost. One must be fully aware that satan has great power and if he can send sickness, he can heal sickness. **These miracles are 'lying wonders' because once satan heals or 'delivers', he has been given a 'doorway' for controlling the person's spiritual man. Once you allow anyone to lay hands on you, you are opening yourself to the 'power' in them.**

Further these 'workers of miracles' will use the Name of Jesus and scripture to back up their campaigns. What you will notice if you listen carefully, is that there will be little or no talk about **Our Resurrected Lord**, nor about the fact that **Jesus Saves**. For example, there is one television 'miracle worker' who blows on people and they fall, who also throws his hand or waves his hand over people and they fall. He never asks for 'decisions for Christ'. He only deals with apparent 'miracles' which look and seem authentic.

Additionally, many Christians have been satisfied (with themselves) too long, without realizing 'spiritual pride' and 'spiritual ignorance' have taken root in their minds. Their tenure of service in their churches, their titles and positions of influence somehow seem to make these persons feel invincible against deception. Satan's mind game have these persons:

1. Not knowing it is possible to be deceived.
2. Thinking God will prevent believer from being deceived.
3. Saying "I am safe under the blood", without intelligent knowledge of the conditions.
4. Saying "I have no sin".
5. Saying "I am doing all that God wants, so all must be right"; without seeking to understand what the will of the

Lord is (Ephesians 5:10-17).[18]

Sometimes the older, supposedly mature, Christian can be open to various types **'lying spirits'**. The long-time member will be faithful to God and support the church but will become <u>bound in the church</u> because of satan's specially tailored 'devices'. Simply put, satan will send the saint a **'spirit of rejection'** (which leads to **'resentment'** and **'rebellion'**),[19] by manipulating their thoughts (and emotions) believe (and feel) that they are being ignored because of their age. Once this older saint agrees with these suggestions from satan, **'self-pity'**, **'rejection'** and **'loneliness'** take over and satan has taken advantage of the long time faithful saint.

Obviously, satan is not going to present a blueprint to each Christian which he has specially designed according to each person's personality, weakness and social situation (so that the person will be aware of his/her potential for failure). Satan usually operates in the area of your innocence, so that 'offenses' come <u>to you</u>. **He then reasons with you**, through your 'flesh' or emotions, about those 'offenses'. While experiencing the hurts and/or disappointment, **satan will manipulate your mind** to dwell on the injustice and unfairness. **While agreeing with these spiritually damaging thoughts, some demons of 'bitterness', 'anger', 'self-righteousness' and, perhaps, even a little 'revenge' may enter.** This is the war that is always, in one form or another, going on in our 'members' (Romans 7:23). **HOW OFTEN HAVE YOU SEEN BITTERNESS AND MEANNESS IN OLDER 'SAINTS' OR CHURCH MEMBERS THAT IS USUALLY DIRECTED TOWARDS THE YOUNG PEOPLE OR NEW MEMBERS?**

---

[18] <u>WAR ON THE SAINTS</u> by Jesse Penn-Lewis, p99.

[19] For a detailed discussion of the ripple affect of the 'spirit of rejection', read <u>Rejection, The Ruling Spirit,</u> by Dr. Fay Ellis Butler.

And since man is not dumb or stupid, **satan will create or use 'devices' to hinder, prevent or stop the Christian.**

The word **'device'** in the King James text (II Corinthians 2:11) is translated from the word **'noemo'** which means **'thoughts'**, **'purposes'**, **'designs'**. In other words, a **'scheme'** or a **'trick'**. The idea of **'device'** or **'trick'** is **that which allows the mind to focus erroneously on an act or problem, with subsequent erroneous conclusions -- THE MIND GAME.**

There was a man in the church at Corinth who was caught as a fornicator who willingly repented to the Church (I Corinthians 5; II Corinthians 2:7). But some in this Corinthian church, perhaps out of embarrassment, hurt, anger and/or resentment, refused to forgive him. Paul was telling the church to forgive him because, if they did not, satan would take advantage of their 'spirit of unforgiveness'.

> *"If anyone has caused grief, he has not so much grieved me as he has grieved all of you, to some extent... The punishment inflicted on him by the majority is sufficient for him. Now instead, you ought to forgive him and comfort him, so that he will not be overwhelmed by excessive sorrow. I urge you, therefore, to reaffirm your love for him. The reason I wrote unto you was to see if you would stand the test and be obedient in everything. If you forgive anyone, I also forgive him. And what I have forgiven -- if there was anything to forgive -- I have forgiven in the sight of Christ for your sake, in order that satan MIGHT NOT OUTWIT US.* **FOR WE ARE NOT UNAWARE OF HIS SCHEMES** *(II Corinthians 2:5-11, NIV).*

Remember, satan can not operate in the spiritual man but only in the carnal. The spiritual man keeps his mind on the Lord and in the word.[20]

---

[20] **Philippians 4:8.**

When unforgiveness is given a place in a Christian's heart, he is open to those 'spirits' or evil forces that work with 'unforgiveness', that is, 'anger', 'resentment', 'hostility', 'bitterness', 'revenge', etc., etc., etc. (See Chapter 3). That is why the Word states, "... to be carnally minded is death..."(Romans 8:6). Satan will make that **self-righteous Christian feel justified withholding sympathy, love and forgiveness from someone who somehow failed and/or hurt him/her.** This is a 'scheme' or 'device' that **satan works in the unforgiving Christian. Honoring seeds of unforgiveness, bitterness, jealousy, self-pity, is 'giving place to the devil' in the mind.** The holding of hurts and personal pain is a work of the flesh reinforced by 'the evil one'. This is 'minding the things of the flesh' rather than things of the Spirit. Notice how the Word seeks to aid the Christian in avoiding this 'device' of satan...

"Brethren, if a man be overtaken in a fault, ye which are spiritual, restore such an one in the spirit of meekness, considering thyself, lest thou also be tempted" (Gal. 6:1).

This does not necessarily mean the saint may be tempted to commit the same sin, but that satan will overtake the individual through 'unforgiveness' and 'self-righteousness'. It is no wonder Galatians 6:3 states, *"For, if a man think himself to be something when he is nothing, he deceiveth himself".*[21]

<u>**God has given us the power and strength to discipline our minds.**</u>

The major battles for your peace and your soul are the subtle and open attacks against the mind. Over and over, again the Bible encourages us to discipline and renew our minds in the Word. God will give any and all persons over to

---

[21] **Compare Isaiah 64:6.**

a reprobate mind who continually refuse to honor God morally and spiritually (See Romans 1:28). As Christians, the concept of renewing your mind according Romans 12:2, of necessity must include a myriad of methods:

- As individuals, the Word of God must be <u>heard, received, meditated upon, studied and memorized.</u>
- As a group, the Body of Christ must become more and more sophisticated in method and approach when teaching, advocating and propagating the Word of God.
- All individuals and groups in the Body of Christ must discipline themselves to spend more time in fasting and prayer.

This is the only way we can assure ourselves of salvation, protect our minds, values and church culture. Repeatedly, we are given the formula for peace and spiritual success.

"Let the Word of Christ dwell in you richly..." (Colossians 3:16).

"Be renewed in the spirit of your mind..." (Ephesians 4:24).

"Thy Word is a lamp unto my feet..." (Psalms 119:105).

*"Therefore, prepare your **minds for** action... As obedient children, do not conform to the evil desires you had when you lived in ignorance" (I Peter 1:13,14 NIV).*

The Christian, because of the Holy Spirit dwelling in the inner man, is equipped to control his/her mind. Once the individual has submitted him/herself to God, he/she can rebuke and resist anything satan sends (James 4:7). This is done by quoting scriptures, singing praises, reading the Bible or a good worthwhile book. **You can discipline your mind.**

"Thou will keep him in perfect peace whose mind is stayed on thee because he trusteth in thee" (Isaiah 26:3)

"Thy Word have I hidden in my heart that I might not sin against thee" (Psalms 119:11).

Remember satan oppresses the mind with thoughts that you believe are yours. . **You are saved, not by feelings or thoughts or ideas, but because you repented, turned from sin and agreed with the Word of God.**

*"My fear is that, just as the serpent seduced Eve by his cunning, your **THOUGHTS MAY BE CORRUPTED** and you may fall away from your sincere and complete devotion to Christ"* (II Cor. 11:3, New America Version).

When you study the Word, memorize the Word, meditate on the Word, satan will not be able to manipulate you through the thoughts that he sends. The Holy Ghost and the Word of God in you will help you to recognize the satan's demons trying to use the 'voice of your mind'.

Man has choices. Being 'made in the image God' means that man determines his relationship with God and other persons. The choices come through the mind (the soul), which determines whether or not man will allow the Spirit of God to rule.

THE BATTLE IS IN THE MIND.

SELF-EXAMINATION
THE MIND GAME

1. Do you run to the latest crusade in town?

2. Do you find yourself longing for someone to give you 'a word'?

3. When you feel depressed, do you act depressed?

4. When you feel angry, do you 'just have to get it off your chest'?

5. Do you 'resist the devil' regularly by identifying the problem, (repenting, if necessary) and then rebuking him?

6. Do you understand that 'flashbacks' which may be painful, will come up from the past?

7. Do you understand that in spite of the past, what you may feel, that you are saved based on your repentance and living in agreement with the Word of God?

9. Do you realize satan will be completely faithful to his job, to destroy you anyway that he can?

10. Do you understand that God allows those valley experiences, during which satan works harder on your faith and confidence?

11. Do you find yourself annoyed with the spiritually fragile Christian, who regularly repents for the same sin?

12. Do you believe that you could never be deceived?

13. Does God 'accept' all of your church work?

SANCTIFICATION, A LIFETIME PROCESS

"Let not sin therefore reign in your mortal body that ye should obey it in the Lusts thereof. Neither yield ye your members as instruments of unrighteousness unto sin: but yield yourselves unto God, as those that are alive from the dead, and your members as instruments of righteousness unto God" (Romans 6:12,13).

When the Christian confesses his/her sins, forsake his/her sins, and invites the Holy Spirit to abide within, he/she is freed from **the penalty of sin (hell)** and from **the power of sin (satan)**. However he/she is still in the world, with the same personality, the same home, the same job, same friends, and the same tendencies. The desire to please God is new, but satan is the same. Therefore, every Christian must actively work at being and remaining 'new'. For example, some friendships must be terminated and some personality traits (like impatience) must be brought under the subjection of the Holy Ghost.

The Christian hears the Word, accepts the Word, makes a decision and then repents. These are acts of the mind. The yielding of the will and the surrendering to God allowed the Lord to come in man's spirit -- The New Birth. **'Sanctification' simply means the process of cleansing or making pure.**

"Having therefore these promises dearly beloved, <u>let us</u> cleanse ourselves from all filthiness of the flesh and spirit, perfecting holiness in the fear of God (II Corinthians 7:1).

Satan is fully aware of the areas of your past vulnerability and consequently sends temptations to the flesh and mind. **Sanctification brings spiritual growth, faith and the strength to resist these temptations.**

In every saint's daily life, new situations call forth new internal and external responses. Not all of these responses are in tune with the Word. In this age of information the mind is bombarded with books, periodicals, billboards, newspapers, television, video, cassette tapes, etc. The information age is so sophisticated that most Christians are unaware of the subliminal assault on the mind almost all day every day. Notice how often you may start singing or humming a tune that is not really a part of your musical culture, or you begin thinking distasteful, sometimes even obscene, thoughts. Have you ever fallen asleep with the television on and found yourself fighting in your sleep because some scene of violence from the television was bombarding your mind WHILE YOU WERE ASLEEP?

Realized or not, we are being mentally manipulated by the secular world with ideas and suggestions (sexual, violent, occultic and/selfish) which do not edify or help. Further, our values and even lifestyles are being subtilely reworked and reshaped.

Therefore, the saint must daily, not only 'watch and pray' but also examine him/herself, make adjustments and lay aside; in other words, 'die daily'. When the old saints taught, 'it takes time to live HOLY', they meant no saint was going to discover all of the dross, weights and shortcomings in one week or even one year. In fact, the Lord is so merciful, He does not let us at one time, see the entire process of sanctification we must experience.

Yet, the only perfection that God requires and expects of every Christian is that he/she measures up to what he/she has been taught, and what is understood. A "baby" Christian does not know or understand as well as someone who has been saved 15 years. Therefore, that individual's walk with the Lord may not seem to be consecrated to a Christian who has been saved many years, BUT GOD ACCEPTS IT. Obviously then, your sanctification is directly related to how you prayerfully listen to the Word, study the Word and commit the Word to your mind and heart and then LIVE BY THE WORD (Psalms 119:11).

"Wherefore lay apart all filthiness and superfluity of naughtiness and receive with meekness the engrafted Word, Which is able to save your souls. But be ye doers of the Word, and not hearers only, deceiving your own selves" (James 1:21,22).

Sanctification is a process the individual Christian must initiate and perpetuate. The Lord has always required His people to cleanse themselves because He is Holy...

"For I AM THE LORD YOUR GOD: Ye shall therefore sanctify yourselves, and ye shall be holy; for I am Holy... for I am the Lord that bringeth you up out of the land of Egypt, to be your God: Ye shall therefore be holy, for I am Lord" (Lev. 11:44,45).

However, because God is so merciful and kind, he makes many provisions for our sanctification. In other words, our sanctification comes by several methods:

1. YOURSELF !!!

"Beloved, now we are the sons of God, and it doth not yet appear what we shall be: but we know that, when he shall appear, we shall be like him; for we shall see him as he is. AND EVERY MAN THAT HATH THIS HOPE IN HIM PURIFIETH HIMSELF, EVEN AS HE IS PURE" (I John 3:2,3).

Externally

a) **Sanctification is laying aside EVERY weight** (Heb. 12:1).

"Dearly beloved, I beseech you as strangers and pilgrims, abstain from fleshly lusts, which war against the soul" *(I Peter 2:11).*

Weights are anything that stop or retard your growth in God. Are you able to watch the 'soaps' on television for 3 hours straight and then pray through? Most of what comes on television glorifies fornication, adultery, murder, drinking, smoking, the occult and even homosexuality. Watching four or five hours of television every day, attenuates or weakens Biblical Christianity.

In other words, television can be a satanic 'brain washing' tool which brings you to the place where mentally and socially you become desensitized, eventually accept (and maybe even partake of) uncleanness. The 'New Age' and other occultic manipulation of the entertainment media should be obvious; e.g, 'Friday the 13th', 'E.T.', 'Ghost', etc. Most of the time the plot, climax and morale of these films are bizarre and ridiculous.

Further, as far fetched as it seems, demon spirits are invading your home when these satanically influenced movies and shows are playing. Sounds ridiculous? Think about the Gospel and religious programs and videos which really honor and magnify God. Don't you feel the presence of God in your home when these are playing? Remember, satan imitates God and creates his own instruments and tools to advance his own kingdom.

Television is just one of many weights that can hinder our growth and freedom. We must be honest with ourselves and with God. **Identify the weights and lay them aside.** You have **a will and powerful decision- making ability;** God is not going to do this for you.

b) **Sanctification is laying aside sins.**
"Mortify therefore your members which are upon the earth; fornication, uncleanness, inordinate affection, evil concupiscence and covetousness, which is idolatry" *(Colossians 3:5).*

Anything that abuses the body is SIN; gluttony, alcoholism, drug addiction, nicotine addiction. Any behavior that affects the Body of Christ negatively is SIN -- sowing discord, fighting, gossiping, etc. (Proverbs 6:16-19). Rebellion (which is as the sin of witchcraft) and stubbornness (which is as iniquity and idolatry) are SINS (I Samuel 15:23). ANY AND ALL sexual activity outside of marriage is SIN AND PERVERSION.

Further, there are many other things we partake of which seem innocuous or harmless, but are SINS. **Submitting to satanic influence or domination such as dabbling in any area of the occult whether it is palm reading, playing with certain games like Dungeons and Dragons or wearing zodiac jewelry, is SIN**[22]. The more innocent some things appear, the more dangerous they are and can become.

Take for example, astrology, which is the study of heavenly bodies with a view towards predicting the course of human affairs. The horoscope craze is ubiquitous. There are columns on astrology in almost 2000 daily papers in the United States. You can purchase books on every aspect of your life for guidance through astrology. ("Astrology for Your Health", "How to Win a Mate Through Astrology", "How to Predict Your Future with Astrology", etc.).

Astrology was devised by the ancient Chaldeans of the Babylonian Empire, a pagan society. They divided the heavens into 12 sections, called the zodiac, and said that the stars controlled the destiny of men. The Chaldeans studied the hour and date a person was born, then predicted his

---

[22] See Ezekiel 13:6,7; Deuteronomy 18:10-14.

destiny. Astrologers believe fate is written in the stars before the individuals birth; and they believe nothing can alter destiny.

Horoscopes and the zodiac (astrology) are satanic tools and an antithesis to Christian doctrine and faith. Unfortunately, many 'born again' Christians adhere to horoscopes, read horoscopes and exchange views with one another. It does not matter how true any horoscope prediction or analysis appears, **it is demonic and a 'doorway' for satan to manipulate and weaken you. This, in fact, allows satan to rule in an area of the mind, when according Romans 12:2, the Christians should be renewing their minds in The Word of God and Prayer.** Just think, how often have you formed your mouth to say "What sign were you born under"? You should answer, "the sign of the Cross of Calvary".

When anyone else begins predicting or analyzing lives and personalities by any other means other than by the Word of God and the revelation of the Holy Spirit, that person is acting as a 'diviner' and using 'divination'.

> "*There shall not be found among you ANYONE...that useth divination, or an observer of the times, or an enchanter, or a witch, or a charmer, or a consulter with familiar spirits, or a wizard, or a necromancer. For ALL THAT DO THESE THINGS ARE AN ABOMINATION UNTO THE LORD*" (Deuteronomy 18:10,11).

Astrology (the horoscope) is an occult practice[23]. If you have been involved in this tool of satan to any extent, you must stop **IMMEDIATELY,** repent, and sanctify yourself of this habit. Stop reading the horoscopes, stop discussing the 'signs' and throw out all books, posters, jewelry and emblems of astrology. Then, **in the name of Jesus of Nazareth, rebuke,**

---

[23] There are other seemingly innocuous occult practices (like reading tea leaves and palm reading), seen most often in carnivals and county fairs.

renounce, bind and cast out that demonic 'horoscope spirit' that manipulated, affected and/or controlled you.

> "The acts of the sinful nature are <u>obvious</u>: sexual immorality, impurity and debauchery; idolatry and witchcraft; hatred, discord, jealousy, fits of rage, self ambition, dissensions, factions and envy; drunkenness, orgies and the like. I warn you, as I did before, that those who live like this will not inherit the kingdom of God" (Galations 5:19-21, NIV).

c) **Sanctification is 'neither giving place to the devil'** (Eph. 4:27) 'and making no provision for the flesh' (Ro. 13:14).

- If you are a saved former alcoholic, you are not going to witness in bars or even attend those alcohol drinking office parties.
- Or, if you are an ex-homosexual, now saved and delivered, you should not take a job as a counselor in a Boy's Home.
- If you were sexually active and single before salvation, you cannot watch or read sexually explicit materials.
- If you have a weak ego, or you were just healed of a weak ego, or just delivered from 'a spirit of vanity', you are not going to start straining and seeking the highest possible position in your organization or church.

d) **Sanctification is 'KEEPING' your tongue** (James 3:6).

> "Death and life are in the power of the tongue and they that love it shall eat the fruit thereof (Proverbs 18:21).

THE POWER OF YOUR LIFE AND THE LIVES OF OTHERS ARE IN YOUR TONGUE!!! Likewise, **the ability to kill is in the tongue; character assassination, the destruction of church unity and church programs.**

The tongue is a very small organ (James 3:2) and will eventually reveal the real person (or the 'inner man'). For out of the abundance of the heart (the motives, intentions and desires), the heart speaketh (Matthew 12:34).

Notice the woman with a "jealous spirit" commenting on a good looking, well-dressed acquaintance, will not be able to give a complete compliment. The 'half-baked' compliment sounds something like this: "I like the outfit but the color looks bad on her", or "she is too old, too hippy, too short or too young for that style". What is in the heart will eventually come out through the mouth. The Bible warns "...*keep thy heart with all diligence" (Proverbs 4:23)*.

Satan will also use subtleties and innuendo with speech to plant seeds of destruction. He will use the truth, the wrong way, to destroy. For example, one woman may tell another that she saw her husband eating lunch with a strange woman three days in one week. This could be true but it have been related to business. A 'seed' has been planted which satan will water.

Speech uttered affects the hearers. Words cannot be retrieved. Listening by the hearers involves the brain--the conscious and subconscious. Even if something spoken seems to be rejected by the hearers, it still penetrates and has some affect. Take a blatant example... If an individual is subjected to ethnic or racial slurs or pejoratives, he/she may control him/herself and refuse to demean him/herself by responding; but internally things begin to happen.

The heart rate increases,
   blood pressure rises,
      head begins to ache while
         ANGER, RAGE and even **HATRED** may enter.

Or, consider the more subtle damaging way words can kill. If a child is criticized all of his life with little or no positive reinforcement, he will never believe in himself, even though he may be a genius, handsome, articulate and talented. His 'inner man' will have been assaulted with so much negativism, for so long, that he accepts low self-esteem, inferiority, and insecurity as his own (and without realizing it).

It is only the ignorant and the foolish who destroy with

their mouths. Positive reinforcement with speech builds; negative, destroys.[24]

The words of a wise man's mouth are gracious; but the lips of a fool will swallow up himself" *(Ecclesiastes 10:12; cf Galatians 6:7).*

On the other hand, God's Words give life, health and deliverance.[25] God used only His Word and spoke the universe into existence. In fact, He honors His Word so, He personified His Word in His own Son (John 1:1). Jesus' Words healed (e.g., the woman with the issue of blood; Matthew 9:20-22), delivered (the man with legion; Mark 5:9-15), and gave life (Lazarus; John 11:43,44). **When we receive His Word, we too, by the 'power of attorney', that is, using the Name of Jesus, can speak words of healing, deliverance and life.**

Further, confession and profession are the basics in holiness. At the outset, you have to, not only believe in thine heart, but confess with thy mouth (Romans 10:9,10). Notice also how often the Bible indicates the importance of professing with your mouth. In Revelation 12:10,11 satan is recorded accusing the saints day and night before God, **'BUT THEY OVERCAME HIM WITH THE BLOOD OF THE LAMB AND THE WORDS OF THEIR TESTIMONY'**. Open confession denies satan the right to manipulate your mind (James 5:16).

"Wholesome Tongue is a Tree of Life (Prov. 15:4).

Your speech (the tongue) must be controlled and

---

[24] If your children and friends are criticized too much, their self-image is weakened. The 'ripple' effect affects you; if you cultivate insecure dependent children, you may have to support them the rest of their lives.

[25] For further information on how God uses the tongue of man, see **APPENDIX I.**

disciplined. **GOD IS NOT GOING TO DO FOR YOU WHAT HE HAS EQUIPPED YOU TO DO FOR YOURSELF.**

"For if ye live after the flesh, <u>ye shall die</u>: but if ye through the Spirit do mortify the deeds of the body, <u>ye shall live</u>" (Romans 8:13).

<u>Internally</u>

a) **<u>The Word of God Sanctifies.</u>**

"Sanctify them through thy truth: Thy Word is Truth (John 17:17).

"Wherewithal shall a young man cleanse his way? by taking heed thereto according to thy Word" (Psalm 119:9).

"I will meditate in thy precepts, and have respect unto thy ways" (Psalm 119:15).

God ordained the ministry of the apostle, prophet, evangelist, pastor and teacher for the perfecting of his people (Ephesians 4:11,12). The tool used in the operation of every ministry is God's Word.

> **The believer must hear the Word.**
> **The believer must meditate on the Word.**
> **The believer must understand the Word.**
> **The believer must memorize the Word.**
> **The believer must hide the Word in his/her heart.**

Every denomination, church or religious group really believes that their interpretation of the Bible and their doctrine is the best. Few denominations or churches distinguish between Bible doctrine and church traditions or culture. Of course, all doctrines in most churches are said to be Bible based. Nevertheless, God has given each individual the Word. After you have been taught and indoctrinated by your local assembly, go home and study and memorize the Word so that it is hidden in the your own heart.

b) **The Holy Ghost sanctifies** (Romans 15:16).

> "...*The comforter will not come unto you; but if I depart, I will send him unto you...Howbeit when he, the Spirit of Truth, is come, he will guide you into all truth...*" *(John 16:7,13).*

The Holy Spirit who abides in the Christian's human spirit will guide and teach the Christian. Since "*...God hath from the beginning chosen you to salvation through sanctification of the Spirit...*" *(II Thessalonians 2:13)*, you grieve the Holy Spirit when He is ignored (Ephesians 4:30). In effect, ignoring the Holy Spirit serves a dispossess notice on Him and He departs. In the words my husband, Rev. John Butler, the Holy Spirit works on you to WORK ON YOURSELF.

Therefore, the saint who is saved and has not been filled with the Holy Ghost has an 'empty house' -- the inner man is cleaned by the Spirit of God but is not filled to overflowing with the Spirit of God. Since the saved-but-not filled saint will not have all the power he/she needs to stay saved, he/she is in danger. Likewise, the once-filled-saint who has not been refilled regularly, has an 'empty house' and is also in danger.

Notice that the empty saint, like an empty house, is doomed for destruction. In the natural sense an empty house, after a period of time, either through neglect or vandalism is no longer inhabitable. The empty house collects dusts and cobwebs. Windows break in times of storm; then the elements, gaining easy access through broken windows, wear down the structures. The house may eventually need a total reconstruction job.

Rare is it that any saint backslides suddenly. The backsliding process is gradual first, with a little bit of discouragement, a little yielding to temptation, staying home from church more often. Then like the decay of an empty house, the backsliding (failure to continuously sanctify oneself) is barely noticeable at first, but later it becomes glaringly evident.

> *"When the unclean spirit is <u>gone out</u> of a man, he walketh through dry places, seeking rest, and findeth none. Then he saith, I will return into my house from whence I came out; and when he is come, he findeth it empty, swept, garnished. Then goeth he, and taketh with himself seven other spirits more wicked than himself, and they <u>enter in</u> and <u>dwell</u> there: and the last state of that man is <u>**worse than the first**</u>" (Matthew 12:43-45).*

Believers will have difficulty remaining saved without the Baptism of the Holy Ghost. On your job, in the streets, in the media, everywhere, the saint is bombarded by evil and his RADAR, his GUIDE, the Holy Ghost must be in operation.

It is the opinion of the writer, that the saint who is saved and does not receive all that God has for him, offends and insults God. If the Holy Ghost is a gift and the gift is not received, then the GIVER may be offended. But thank God, God is long-suffering.

> *"**ASK**, and it shall be given you, seek, and ye shall find; **KNOCK**, and it shall be opened unto you: for **EVERYONE** that asketh receiveth; and that seeketh findeth; and to him that knocketh it shall be opened. Or what man is there of you whom if his son ask bread, will he give him a stone?...If ye being evil, know how to give good gifts unto your children,*

HOW MUCH MORE SHALL YOUR FATHER WHICH IS IN HEAVEN GIVE GOOD THINGS TO THEM THAT ASK HIM" (Matt. 7: 7-9,11).

All too often the 'seeker' becomes discouraged because he/she really 'feels' like his/her best is being done to be filled. **BUT THE HOLY GHOST IS A GIFT** "...*given to them that obey Him*" (Acts 5:32). God is very much aware of the person who believes 'as the scripture has said' (John 7:38) and who has made the total commitment to give the Lord their best on His terms. The earnest totally committed Christian will do whatever is necessary, even fasting and praying three days and nights as part of the surrendering, seeking, and sanctification process. **(The sanctification process begins prior to receiving the Baptism of the Holy Ghost and certainly must continue after receiving the Holy Ghost.)** Further, the Christian will meditate on the Word of God and the goodness of God in order to bring the mind and the will to the point where he/she can believe enough to receive the Gift of the Holy Ghost.

Notice all the reasons the Holy Ghost will not be given (or will leave the once-filled-saint). All of them are related to, or part of, the sanctification process.

1. **Slothfulness, carelessness, sins of omission.**
   "*Therefore to him that knoweth to do good, and doeth it not, to him it is sin*" *(James 4:17).*
   - Failure to read and study the Bible consistently.
   - Failure to attend regular church services consistently.
   - Failure to pay tithes and give offerings consistently.
   - Failure to witness consistently. Etc.

2. **Failure to lay aside weights and sins.**
   "*Wherefore seeing we also are compassed about with so great a cloud of witnesses, let us lay aside every weight, and the sin which doth easily beset us, and let us run with patience the race that is set before us*" (Heb. 12:1).

- Failure to stop the gossiping and backbiting before it begins.
- Failure to give up 'television addiction'.
- Failure to give up 'clothing and jewelry addiction'.
- Failure to deal with eating disorders such as gluttony, and sugar or caffeine addiction.

3. **Failure to WORSHIP GOD.**
   *"For HERE have we no continuing city, but seek one to come. **BY HIM** therefore LET US offer the SACRIFICE OF PRAISE TO GOD   CONTINUALLY, that is, the fruit of our lips giving **thanks to his name** (Hebrews 13: 14,15; cf Psalms 22:3, 100:4).*
- Failure to give Him Glory in Hard times as well as in good times.
- Forgetting and taking for granted the ordinary, e.g., being able to walk, talk, see, eat, etc.
- Failure to get to church on time to praise God in the prayer with the saints.
- Failure to cultivate the spirit of reverence throughout your life.

4. **Failure to love the brethren and to do good to the brethren.**
   *"Beloved, **LET US** love one another... Beloved, if God so loved us, we ought also to love one another. No man hath seen God at any time. If we love one another, **GOD DWELLETH IN US**, and his love is perfected in us" (I John 4:7,11,12).*

   "As we have therefore opportunity, let us do good unto all men, especially unto them who are of the household of faith" (Gal. 6:10).
- Ignoring the needy and elderly.
- Forgetting to visit and pray for the sick and homebound.
- Forgetting to support burdened saints, particularly struggling parents.

- Showing partiality, giving to those who have no need and not giving to those who need.

5. **Fearfulness and unbelief.**
   "For God hath not given us the spirit of fear, but of power, and of love, and of a sound mind" (II Timothy 1:7).
   "But the fearful and unbelieving,....shall have their part in the lake which burneth with fire and brimstone..." (Rev. 21:8).
- Afraid to speak out against the wrong discovered in the church family.
- Afraid to come to church at night.
- Afraid to witness.
- Afraid of satan and demons.

It is the **RIGHT AND RESPONSIBILITY** of every Christian to be filled with the Holy Ghost and remain filled. He/she must do everything within his/her power to please and obey God.

Sanctification is on-going but daily process. Simply put, Christ is Lord and we dare not 'crucify his flesh' again (Hebrews 6:6) nor 'grieve the Holy Spirit'(Ephesians 4:30). We, therefore, continue to watch ourselves -- our thoughts, our conduct, our leisure time activities, our faithfulness, as well as pray. We continue to sanctify ourselves, not only because we fear and reverence God, but also because we want to please the very heart of God. We recognize, in our absolute obedience to God, we are demonstrating our absolute love for Him.

Self-Examination # 3

1. Do you talk on the phone more than 1/2 hour socially each day?

2. Do you witness to souls for just as long as you socialize on the phone each day?

3. When you repent of a weight or a sin, do you give up that weight or sin immediately and permanently?

4. Do you brag or seem to glory in your past sinful life when you testify?

5. Do you watch day and/or night time 'soap operas'?

6. Do you watch more than two hours of non-Gospel television every day?

7. Do you spend as much time studying the Word and praying as you do watching television?

8. Do you read the horoscopes daily?

9. Do you ask people their zodiac sign?

10. Do you read the Bible daily?

11. Do you memorize at least a scripture a month?

12. Do you have more unsaved friends than saved friends?

13. Do you feel more relaxed in the company of your unsaved friends than in the company of the saints?

14. Are you working extremely hard, trying to look good, rushing from 'rags to riches' in a hurry?

WEAPONS AGAINST THE ENEMY

Satan hates God and anyone who lives for God. Satan knows he has to go to hell. He is determined to lie, seduce, deceive, hurt, wound, defile, kill and destroy each of us, our families, our communities and our churches.

"The thief [satan] *cometh not but for TO STEAL, and TO KILL, and TO DESTROY..."(John 10:10).*

"...Your adversary the devil, as a roaring lion, walketh about, seeking WHOM HE MAY DEVOUR" (I Peter 5:8).

However, the saved, (born again) person is protected, and freed from satan's rage because he/she has accepted the provision made for his/her spiritual safety. When Jesus died 'the death of sin' for us, went into a devil's hell, and was risen by the Father in the power of the Holy Ghost, He *'spoiled ALL principalities and powers'* of satan (Colossians 2:15). **The same Holy Ghost power, which resurrected Jesus, renders all demon spirits ineffective through the prayers of the righteous.**
Satan is a refining instrument or tool of God (Romans 8:28). Every victory over the enemy makes the believer more powerful in the warfare. Every victory over the enemy puts more of self to death.
The saints of God are not only protected, but equipped to do battle (since the victory is already won). *"Now thanks be to God, which ALWAYS causeth us to triumph in Christ..."* *(II Corinthians 2:14).* The people of God must live, talk and operate in the arena of confident overcomers and victors and remember the 'carte blanche' to Holy Ghost power Jesus has given us.

*"Behold, I give **UNTO YOU POWER** to tread on <u>serpents</u> and <u>scorpions,</u> and over **ALL** the power of the enemy and nothing shall by any means hurt you (Luke 10:19).*

Every time you fail a test or refuse to go through a trial, satan has a mastery over you in that area of your life. **There are basic weapons, used by believers, which activates the Power of God, and defeats the enemy.** None of these weapons are carnal, but powerful instrumentalities of the immutable Godhead. These weapons are:

1. The Blood of Jesus.
2. The Holy Ghost
3. The Word of God
4. The Name of Jesus
5. Prayer and Intercession
6. Praise and Worship
7. Speaking in 'Other Tongues'

*"The weapons of our warfare are not carnal, but **mighty through God to the pulling down of strongholds..."***
(II Corinthians 10:4).

WEAPONS AGAINST THE ENEMY: THE BLOOD OF JESUS

The **BLOOD OF JESUS** is a weapon against the enemy!
*...For the accuser of our brethren is cast down, which accused them before our God day and night. And they overcame him by the **BLOOD OF THE LAMB**, and the word of their testimony; and they loved not their lives unto the death (Revelations 12:10,11).*

First of all, the **Blood of Jesus** was central to the completed work of redemption; *"...without the shedding of blood, is no remission" (Hebrews 9:22).* Secondly, He, Jesus

Christ, has ransomed all believers from satan's evil powers:

> "*And they sung a new song, saying, Thou art worthy to take the book, and to open the seals thereof: for thou was slain, and hast redeemed us to God by thy **BLOOD** out of every kindred, and tongue, and people and nation*" (Revelation 5:9).

We were dead in our trespasses and sin, and He was the only true Light and Life (John 1:4). Jesus came willingly to die a physical and spiritual death that man might again have spiritual life, that is, be reconciled back to God (Hebrews 9:26).

A) **The BLOOD OF JESUS IS A WEAPON OF POWER BECAUSE IT IS IMPORTANT TO GOD, THE FATHER.**

- **THE BLOOD is an everlasting covenant with God.** When God makes a covenant, it is binding and permanent. "*Wherefore Jesus also, that he might sanctify the people with his own blood, suffered without the gate... Now the God of peace, that brought again from the dead our Lord Jesus, that great shepherd of the sheep through, **THE BLOOD OF THE EVERLASTING COVENANT...**"(Hebrews 13:12,20).*

"*Though he were a Son, Yet learned he obedience by the things which he suffered; And being made perfect, he became the author of eternal salvation unto all them that obey him*" (Hebrews 5:8,9).

As long as the redemptive work of the **Blood of Jesus** is applied to any person's life, he is an 'heir of God' with eternal life that begins immediately.

"*Now it is God who makes both us and you stand firm in Christ. He anointed us, set his seal of ownership on us, and put his Spirit in our hearts as a deposit, GUARANTEEING WHAT IS TO COME" (II Corinthians 1:22, NIV).*

- **THE BLOOD restored the love relationship lost in The Fall in the Garden of Eden** (Ro. 5:12).
*"For it pleased the Father that in him should all fullness dwell; and having made peace through **THE BLOOD OF HIS CROSS**, by him to reconcile all things to himself;... and you, that were sometime alienated and enemies in your mind by wicked works, yet now hath he reconciled in the body of his flesh through death, to present you unblamable and unreproveable in his sight" (Colossians 1:19-22).*

God loved man, the crowning climax of creation, so much that he gave man free choice as well as the capacity for love. The Son, Jesus, loved the Father, so much that He presented Himself to the Father (as **the sacrificial 'Lamb of God'**) in order for man to once again be in a love relationship with God, that is, in a relationship of absolute obedience and reverence.

- **THE BLOOD OF JESUS was the means by which God could give His Spirit to man.** Jesus, shed **HIS BLOOD**, went into the Grave, was resurrected, and ascended back to the Father. The Holy Spirit could then be given to all those who repented and allowed themselves to be cleansed by the **Blood**.
"God has raised this Jesus to life, and we are all witnesses of the fact. Exalted to the right hand of God, he has received from the Father the promised Holy Spirit and has poured out what you now see and hear" (Acts 2:32,33 NIV).

- **The BLOOD OF JESUS** brings deliverance from the judgement of God. Just as in the Old Testament when the children of Israel was protected from the last plague in Egypt by the blood over the doorpost, today the **BLOOD OF JESUS** applied to the saints lives will protect from the wrath of God on judgement day.

"And the blood shall be to you for a token upon the houses where ye are: and when I see the blood, I will pass over you, and the plague shall not be upon you to destroy you, when I smite the land of Egypt" (Exodus 12:13).

B) **The BLOOD OF JESUS IS A WEAPON OF GREAT POWER AND IMPORTANCE TO ALL CHRISTIANS**

- **THE BLOOD OF JESUS is so powerful, it instantly cleanses any sinner who repents.**
  *"But if we walk in the light, as he is in the light, we have fellowship one with another, and **the BLOOD OF JESUS CHRIST** his son cleanseth us from all sin" (I John 1:7).*

  *"For by **one offering** he hath perfected for ever them that are sanctified" (Hebrews 10:14).*

- **THE BLOOD brings each person who receives Christ into the FAMILY OF GOD.**
  *"But now in Christ Jesus, ye who sometimes were far off are made nigh by the **BLOOD OF CHRIST**...Now therefore ye are no more strangers and foreigners, but fellow-citizens with the saints, and of the household of God..." (Ephesians 2:13,19).*

- **THE BLOOD OF JESUS gives daily access to the Power that only abode in the Holy of Holies under the law.**
  *"Therefore, brothers, since we have confidence to enter the Most Holy Place by the **BLOOD OF JESUS**, by a new and living way opened for us through the curtain, that is, his body, and since we have a great priest over the house of God, let us draw near to God with a sincere heart in full assurance of faith..." (Heb. 10:19-22 NIV).*

- **THE BLOOD OF JESUS makes every believer a priest and an intercessor of great power**, because as soon as **the Father recognizes HIS SON'S BLOOD**, which has been applied to the believer's life, He responds.

- **THE BLOOD OF JESUS makes every believer a 'king' to rule in the spiritual realm wherever the believer is located (at home. in church, on the job, or in the street).**
  "...*Unto him that loved us, and washed us from our sins in his own BLOOD, And hath made us kings and priests unto God and His Father; to him be glory and dominion for ever and ever*" *(Revelations 1:5,6).*

  The **BLOOD OF JESUS** gives divine and direct access to the very throne and presence of God at any time and at all times (Hebrews 4:15,16; Matthew 18:18). This is what Martin Luther called 'the priesthood of all believers', which is a basic and universal principle of Holiness.

C) **The BLOOD OF JESUS IS A WEAPON OF GREAT POWER AND IMPORTANCE TO satan.**

- Satan knows there is no contest with **THE BLOOD OF JESUS.** Satan **MUST RETREAT FROM THE POWER OF THE BLOOD OF JESUS.**
  "*And they overcame him by the BLOOD OF THE LAMB, and the word of their testimony; and they loved not their lives unto the death*" *(Revelations 12:11).*

  The word "overcame" derives from the Greek word 'nikao' which means 'the mightiest prevail'. Therefore, satan may affect possessions, the physical body and even relatives, but he cannot stop the **BLOOD** washed saint, whose mind has been made up to serve Christ at any cost.

- Satan knows that Jesus was **the Divine Perfect Sinless**

Sacrifice for our sins, in complete obedience to His Father's will. Notice that satan was pleased to keep the children of Israel in various states of rebellion and disobedience. All the thousands of bullocks, rams, lambs, goats, doves, pigeons could only make His people ceremonially clean for worship; these sacrifices gave the individual no power over sin and satan.

"But those sacrifices are an annual reminder of sins, because it is impossible for the bulls and goats to take away sins...Day after day every priest stands and performs his religious duties; again and again he offers the same sacrifices, which can never take away sins. **But when THIS PRIEST** (Jesus) **had offered for all time one sacrifice for sins,** *he sat down at the right hand of God...because by one sacrifice he has made perfect, forever those who are being made holy"* (Hebrews 10:3,11,12.14, NIV).

Satan hates it when the people of God yield to Christ, **The Lamb of God**, in complete obedience to the will of the Father. Sin and satan is then absolutely powerless in the lives of the **'BLOOD-washed'** saints.

- Satan knows that **'BLOOD-washed' saint** is empowered by the Holy Ghost and therefore has no fear of him (II Tim 1:7). Satan knows when the saints pray **'COVER US WITH YOUR BLOOD'** and **'LET YOUR BLOOD PREVAIL**, that he is powerless before the servant of God.

Recognize, however, that the **Power of THE BLOOD OF JESUS** is effective **ONLY** when an individual has submitted to regeneration by the **BLOOD OF JESUS**. Satan and his demons operate in the spiritual realm and they can 'see' the **BLOOD OF JESUS** in the lives of the saints. Therefore, when **'Blood-washed' child of God**, prays **'THE BLOOD OF JESUS'** satan must retreat.

However, satan and his demons, when the 'stakes' are high enough, may attempt to hold on to his territory through deception. More than a few times, I have witnessed persons who were demon possessed, saying **THE BLOOD OF JESUS**, just like the praying saints. The difference is that when the demon spirit is speaking (even if sounds like the voice of the person), the intonations are flat and trancelike. In addition, if it is a demon speaking, the demon **will not say**, "**Jesus is my Resurrected Lord**". Even if satan does attempt diversionary tactics by imitating the saints, he cannot withstand **THE BLOOD OF JESUS** and the prays of the saints for too long.

WEAPONS AGAINST THE ENEMY: THE HOLY GHOST

The HOLY GHOST is a WEAPON against the Enemy.

Remember, **THE HOLY GHOST** is the executive agent in the earth, operating in and through the believer, carrying out the PLAN OF SALVATION in the earth (Acts 1:8; Matthew 28: 19; Mark 16:16-20). The Holy Ghost operates in and through the believer to reprove the world of sin, convict the world of Christ's righteousness and warn the world of the coming judgement (John 16:8-12). Believers are 'ambassadors for Christ' (II Corinthians 5:20), qualified by **HOLY GHOST**.

The **HOLY GHOST** has many works;
a)   He brings salvation; John 3:5-8.
b)   He sanctifies; Ro. 15:16, I Cor. 6:11, II Thess. 2:13.
c)   He teaches; John 14:26, I John 2:27.
d)   He delivers; Mark 16:16,17.
e)   He baptizes the saints and he fills; Acts 2:4.
f)   He baptizes believers into the Body of Christ;
      I Cor. 12:13.

Each of these works happens in the believer as he/she yields him/herself to the presence and power of the **HOLY GHOST**. God executes His Will in the earth through **HOLY GHOST FILLED** believers. In John 14:16, Jesus told his followers that He would give them another Comforter (the **HOLY GHOST), 'A Paraclete'** (or 'someone who is called along side to help, as well as counsel and direct'). Interestingly, 'advocate' in I John 2:1 where Jesus is called our Advocate with the Father, is derived from the same Greek Word, 'parakletos'.

- The **HOLY GHOST** is an ever-present Comforter, Teacher and Guide because he is perpetually available (in the inner man) (John 14:26).

- The **HOLY GHOST** in the believer will instruct as well as protect the believer in extreme circumstances of satanic attack. He will warn you against danger and minister during sleep -- in dreams (Acts 21:4).

- More than that, in extreme crises and stress, those times when we don't know how to pray, the **HOLY GHOST** Himself will take up our moans and interpret and plead before God for us; He makes intercession for the faithful. The Holy Ghost can interpret your pain through your groans and carry the message to the Father (Romans 8:26,27).

- Further, if you cannot even groan, the **HOLY GHOST** will stir another saint hundreds of miles away to pray for you **(even though they do not know the problem** Acts 9:10-18).

Unfortunately, all too often, Christians speak of evil forces operating in the world through satan, 'the prince of this world', as though he is invincible.

Satan is <u>not invincible</u>:
1. **Satan's defeat is already assured.**
   "...God made you alive with Christ...And having disarmed the powers and authorities, he made a public spectacle of them, triumphing over them by the cross" (Colossians 2:14,15, NIV).

2. **As a joint-heir with Christ, you have already been given POWER to defeat satan.**
   *"Behold I give unto you **POWER** to tread on serpents and scorpion, and over <u>all the power of the enemy</u>: and nothing shall by any means hurt you"* (Luke 10:19).

3. **It is the responsibility of each born again believer to exercise the POWER that has already been given.**
   *"I pray also that the eyes of your heart may be enlightened in order that you may know the hope to which he has called you...**and his incomparably great power for us who believe. That power is like the working of his mighty strength, which he exerted in Christ when he raised him from the dead and seated him at his right hand in heavenly realms, far above all rule and authority, power, and dominion**..."* (Ephesians 1:18-21, NIV).

4. **It is every believer's right to be strengthened with more POWER as the believer works consistently for God.**
   "Now unto Him that is able to do exceeding abundantly above all that we ask or think, according to the power that worketh within us" (Eph. 3:20).

Therefore as Baptized and filled believers, heirs of God and joint-heirs with Christ, in the kingdom of heaven[26], we are kings and queens who have the right...

---

[26] Read Matthew 13 for a description of the kingdom of heaven.

- To issue decrees (Job 22:28):
- To proclaim salvation (Matt. 28:19); and
- To tear down strongholds of satan (II Cor. 10:4).

The **HOLY GHOST** is a weapon because there is no victory without Him, and because nothing will happen if you do not use what you have.

> *"When the enemy shall come in like a flood, **the Spirit of the Lord** shall lift up a standard against him (Isaiah 59:19).*

A **'standard'** in ancient warfare was like the a country's flag today. The **'standard'** was always carried in front of the attacking force; as long as the enemy saw the **'standard'** coming towards them, the enemy knew that they had not overpowered the opposing forces. Satan is continuously working through and with his hierarchy of evil demons and dominions. Each born again believer must recognize his/her responsibility in keeping the already defeated enemy defeated (before satan makes spiritual inroads on our peace and Power).

In today's warfare against the enemy, **the Spirit of the Lord (THE HOLY GHOST) lifts up a standard against satan.**

- **The standard of the HOLY GHOST** is lifted up when the presence of evil is powerful enough for you to be physically sensitive-- sometimes becoming nauseous because of witchcraft, homosexuality, hatred or some terribly abominable spirit in your presence. The Lord means for you to respond with **warfare prayer!**

- **The standard of the HOLY GHOST** is lifted when the Lord gives you a dream or vision about something that satan is planning against you.

Example

When my third child (who is now in his thirties, an ordained elder, and married with three children) was an infant of about 8 months old, I had a frightening dream. In the dream he had slipped while trying to pull himself up in the bathtub, banged his head, became unconscious and drowned. At that time being so busy, as a mother, housewife, and nurse working nights, I was always trying to save time. I would place my children in their bath water with toys to keep them busy for awhile. Sometimes the two older children would scramble out and leave the baby in the tub.

That dream was so real and so frightening, that not only I began bathing them in much less water, I never left them to play in the tub alone. Looking back I realize that satan's strategy was to cause something to happen that would troubled me with oppression by the demon spirits 'guilt' and 'grief' for the rest of my life.

- **The standard of the HOLY GHOST** is lifted up when the Lord instructs another Christian to minister to you in some way (it may be just a warning by phone).

Example

One of the saints in living in one of the New England States (the seat bed of satanism), who has been warring against the forces of darkness, received a call at 3:30 in the morning from another Christian. The caller stated, "*The Lord told me to tell you and your husband to get up and pray throughout your house*". Immediately the couple began praying throughout the house, when they arrived in the back of the house, powerful oppressive demon forces met them. They immediately began rebuking, binding and dispossessing, the evil out of their house. The Lord instructed them to anoint all the windows and doors with oil and walk around the property, pray and drop oil, to seal the place against the enemy.

One of the saints had previously warned her to pray and to anoint her children every day before sending them off to school.

- **The standard of the HOLY GHOST is lifted** when the Lord turns certain danger away.

Example
One of God's dedicated, committed evangelists living in Chicago, Illinois, arrived home from church very late one night. As he was parking his car, two armed men approached him with the obvious intention of robbing, maybe even killing him. SUDDENLY, the two men turned and ran like wild lions were chasing them. The man of God turned around and looked. He saw two eight feet tall, bronze men, with army colored trench coats marching toward him. THEY WERE ANGELS. They stopped beside him until he entered his home. By the time, he called his wife to come and look, they were gone.

When we pray for the **HOLY GHOST 'to lift up a standard'**, we are acknowledging that we are in a 'partnership of victory' with the Lord and are that we are fulfilling all of our responsibility. *"But he that is joined to the Lord is one Spirit" (I Corinthians 6:17).*
God will open your spiritual eyes and train you how to maintain the victory in every area of the warfare.

*"Now we have received, not the spirit of the world, but the **SPIRIT** which is of God; that we might know the things that are freely given to us of God" (I Cor. 2:12).*

"But the anointing which ye have received of him abideth in you, and ye need not that any man teach you: but as the same anointing teacheth you of all things, and is truth, and is no lie, and even as it hath taught you, ye shall abide in him" (I John 2:27).

The **HOLY GHOST** is always working to keep the body healed and individuals holy.

WEAPONS AGAINST THE ENEMY: THE WORD OF GOD

The Word of God is a Weapon against the enemy
*"The **WORD OF GOD** is **QUICK** and **POWERFUL**, and **SHARPER THAN ANY TWO EDGED SWORD**, piercing even to the dividing asunder of soul and spirit, and of the joints and marrow, and is a <u>discerner of thoughts and the intents of the heart</u> (Hebrews 4:12)*

*"Is not **MY WORD** like as a fire? saith the Lord; and like a hammer that breaketh a rock to pieces?" (Jer. 23:29).*

A <u>hammer</u>, <u>fire</u>, and <u>an incomparable two edged sword</u> are powerful images or metaphors, depicting the power of the **WORD** to build faith **IN THE POWER OF THE WORD**.
Jesus is the WORD made flesh. He is actually the personal and personified **WORD OF GOD** because Christ, as 'THE WORD,' reveals the heart and mind of God. Jesus as **THE WORD** was also **THE WORD WITH GOD**, demonstrating His own preexistence. This preexistent power, which was recorded in Genesis, documents the Godhead **speaking** a perfect creation into existence.

"In the past God spoke to our forefathers through the prophets at many times and in various ways, but in these last days he has spoken to us by his son, who he

appointed heir of all things and <u>through whom he made the universe</u>" (Hebrews 1:1,2, NIV).

THE WORD OF GOD used by a person filled with the Holy Ghost is an incontestable force. Did not satan tempt Jesus several times who answered satan with **THE WORD OF GOD**, "*It is written, man shall not live by bread alone...*".

"*It is written again, thou shalt not tempt the Lord thy God*".

"*Get thee hence satan: for it is written, Thou shalt worship the Lord the God, and him only shalt thou serve*" (Matt. 4:3-11)

JESUS, WHO IS THE WORD, used **THE WORD OF GOD** as a weapon. For the scripture states:

"*THEN THE DEVIL LEAVETH HIM...*" (Matt.4:11).

THE WORD OF GOD is a weapon of GREAT POWER because the Lord backs up **HIS OWN WORD**, (when it is used by the saints) with results.

"*Verily I say unto you, Whatsoever ye shall bind on earth shall be bound in heaven, and whatsoever ye shall loose on earth shall be loosed in heaven*" (Matt. 18:18).

However individuals can be set free from possession by demons with **THE WORD OF GOD**.

Example

I was called on to minister to a person who was apparently possessed with Legion (Mark 5:8-13) because an evil spirit spoke out and said, "*I did not stay in the swine*". Another spirit spoke out in <u>another</u> voice and said, "I crucified Jesus". (This all occurred the Saturday before Easter.) The Lord immediately attacked this lie with, "*O death, where is thy sting? O*

grave, where is thy victory?" (I Cor. 15:55). "*For I delivered unto you first of all that which I also received how that Christ died for our sins according to the scriptures, and that he was buried and that he rose again the third day according to the scriptures*" *(I Cor. 15:3,4).*

For every lie that each of those demons spoke out of the woman, the Lord defeated the already defeated foe with scripture. "*Is not my word like as a fire: saith the Lord; and like a hammer that breaketh the rock in pieces?*" *(Jer. 23:29)* came alive. Those demons, visibly squirming and flinching, would retreat from the eyes of this woman for longer and longer periods while the lies were bombarded with scripture. Demons were obviously fleeing while the Lord had me quoting scriptures.

Finally, the woman gained control of her mind and tongue and wanted all the demons out; she began to repeat every scripture the Lord gave to her to repeat. The Lord gave four verses from Psalm 51.

"*Create in me a clean heart, O God and renew a right spirit within me.*

Cast me not away from thy presence and take not thy holy spirit from me.

Restore unto me the joy of thy salvation; and uphold me with thy free spirit.

Then will I teach transgressors thy ways; and sinners shall be converted unto thee" *(Psalm 51:10-13).*

At first a 'stubborn demon' would keep her lips pressed together so that she could not quote these scriptures. The Lord simply had me to state THE

BLOOD OF JESUS RELEASES YOUR MOUTH TO SAY "..........". At first this had to be done for each Word. Over and Over again these scriptures were quoted until she could repeat them, a sentence at a time, without interference by demons. For four hours the Lord used His own Word with this soul until she was no longer possessed. By her own testimony, she acknowledged that she could see everything and hear everything but she had no control over her actions or speech. However, she said she felt the demons trembling with fear inside of her when the scriptures were being quoted. With each scripture she felt a cleansing soothing presence flowing through her body.

Everyone in the room realized that the deliverance was almost complete when she was able to quote scriptures with ease. Chaplain Barbara Williams Sr. told me to ask her what else there. She immediately told us 'selfishness', and 'the lack of love'. I ask her about 'rebellion'. She cried out "*That's it*". I told her to ask the Lord to forgive her for all these. We ended this deliverance session with Romans 8:1,2; "*There is therefore now no condemnation to them which are in Christ Jesus, who walk not after the flesh, but after the Spirit. For the law of the Spirit of life in Christ Jesus hath made me free from the law of sin and death*".

Approximately one third of the ministry of Jesus was delivering people from demons. Notice how!
Matthew 8:16 states specifically that "*...he cast out spirits with HIS WORD...*". Further, in the Psalms you will find "*He sent HIS WORD and healed them, and delivered them from their destructions*"
(Psalm 107:20).
The Word of God is a weapon of **GREAT POWER** because **the Lord backs up his own WORD** with results, when

81

it is used by individuals who have allowed the Holy Spirit to reside (abide) in 'the inner man'. The Lord told Jeremiah who was fearful of the people, "...*I will hasten MY WORD to perform it*" *(Jeremiah 1:12).*

In order to use the word effectively, you must:
- Get in **THE WORD** (Isaiah 34:16).
- Live by **THE WORD** (Jeremiah 15:16; John 17:17).
- Let **THE WORD OF GOD** build you up (Acts 20:32).
- Let **THE WORD** be your guide and light (Psalm 119:105,130).

God has given us **THE WORD** as a weapon. If we are saved and sincere enough about our salvation to fast and pray and bind **THE WORD** in our hearts, we will become very effective in the warfare against Satan.

However, obtaining a command of **THE WORD** is work.
1. You must study **THE WORD** (John 5:39).
2. You must meditate on **THE WORD** (Ps.119:97).
3. You must memorized **THE WORD** (Ps. 119:11).[27]
4. You must attend Sunday School.
5. You must attend Bible Study to be taught.

Further, you must learn to check the many things you hear and see with **THE WORD**. Even if you do believe actually the Lord is giving you a "Word" through someone, does what you hear agree with **the written Word of God**? Jesus himself instructed to be sure of yourself as to who you are in God;

> "*Search the Scriptures; for in them ye think ye have eternal life: and they are they which testify of me*" *(John 5:39).*

---

[27] See Appendix III for some techniques for Bible memorization.

Using **THE WORD OF GOD** as a weapon, whether by preaching, teaching or casting out devils, means that you <u>must</u> spend time **IN THE WORD.**

"And these words ...shall be in thine heart:...and thou shall talk of them when thou sittest in thine house, when thou walkest by the way, and when thou liest down, and when thou risest up..."(Deuteronomy 6:6,7).

When you testify aloud according to what **THE WORD** says you are, you are serving notice on satan that he is defeated. Obviously you must know and commit to your heart and mind what and who **THE WORD OF GOD** states that you are.

Everyday testify aloud to yourself and satan one or all of the following scriptures:

I AM 'a new creature' (II Corinthians 5:17).

I AM 'a son of God' (John 1:12; I John 3:1,2; Romans 8:14).

I AM 'an ambassador for Christ' (II Corinthians 5:20).

I AM 'the righteousness of God in Jesus' (II Cor. 5:21).

I AM 'an heir of God' (Romans 8:17).

I AM 'a joint-heir with Christ' (Romans 8:17).

I AM 'full of power' (Micah 3:8; Acts 1:8; Luke 10:19).

I AM 'protected' (Psalm 34:7; 23:3; Isaiah 54:17).

I AM 'prosperous'(Joshua 1:8; Psalm 1:2,3; 3 John 2).

I AM 'never alone' (Job 5: 19-22; Hebrews 13:5).

I AM 'an overcomer' (I John 5:4,5).

I AM 'an intercessor' (I John 5:14,15; Jer. 33:3).

I AM 'more than a conqueror' (Romans 8:37).

One thing is certain if you live according to **THE WORD** and testify constantly according to **THE WORD, YOU CANNOT FAIL.**

> *"But, **THE WORD OF THE LORD** endureth forever... (I Peter 1:25).*
> *"Forever, O Lord, **THY WORD** is settled in heaven (Ps. 119:89).*
> *"Heaven and earth shall pass away, but **MY WORDS** shall not pass away" (Matthew 24:35).*

Satan does not want **THE WORD OF GOD** in your heart (mind) and will do everything he can to keep you from renewing your mind in **THE WORD** (Romans 12:2); for example, notice how quickly and often you find yourself falling asleep while trying to study the Bible.

It should be evident and obvious that if you obey **THE WORD,** live according to **THE WORD,** speak **THE WORD,** you will abide forever. **THE WORD OF GOD USED BY AN ANOINTED SAINT OF GOD IS POWERFUL!**

> *"And take the helmet of salvation, and the <u>sword of the SPIRIT</u>, which is the **WORD OF GOD**" (Eph 6:17).*

WEAPONS AGAINST THE ENEMY: THE NAME OF JESUS

THE NAME OF JESUS IS A WEAPON AGAINST THE ENEMY!

JESUS means 'Jehovah is Salvation' as well as 'Deliverer'. **THE NAME OF JESUS** represents the awesome **Power** of the entire Godhead.

"...Which he wrought in Christ, when he raised him from the dead, and set him at his own right hand in the heavenly places, Far above all principality, and power, and might, and dominion, and every name that is named, not only in this world, but also in that which is to come" (Eph.1:20,21).

The Power in **THE NAME OF JESUS** is so great that calling on **HIS NAME** saves.

"Neither is there salvation in any other: for there is none other NAME under heaven given among men, whereby we must be saved" (Acts 4:12).

*"For whosoever call upon **THE NAME OF THE LORD** shall be saved" (Romans 10:13).*

HIS NAME is so great that disciples were healing the sick and casting out devils **IN THE NAME OF JESUS** before Jesus was crucified, resurrected and ascended back to His father (Mark 9:38-39). Even satan recognized the power of **THE NAME OF JESUS** and sent out demonic deceivers **using the NAME OF JESUS** (Matt. 24:5).

- **The Authority in THE NAME OF JESUS**
  Authority refers to the right to use **THE NAME** as well What and Who backs up **THE NAME**. It is similar to the legal 'power of attorney' which allows a surrogate to conduct business and legal affairs for a person who is not physically present.

  This **Authority** was instantaneous and complete at the moment of your new birth, for *"as many as received him,*

85

to them gave he **Power** to become sons of God, even **TO THEM THAT BELIEVE ON HIS NAME...**" *(John 1:12)*. And because Jesus submitted himself in absolute obedience to the Father that we may be reconciled back to the Father, we are given the right and the **Authority** to come to the Father praying **IN THE NAME OF JESUS.**

"And in that day ye shall ask me nothing. Verily, Verily, I say unto you, Whatsoever ye shall ask the Father IN MY NAME, he will give it you. Hitherto have ye asked nothing in MY NAME: ask, and ye shall receive, that your joy may be full" (John 16:23,24).

- **The Power in THE NAME OF JESUS**
Power refers to force, strength, and might. The Power of the name of Jesus and the **Power** behind **THE NAME OF JESUS** cannot be separated. They are one and the same. You will observe in scripture that *'JESUS'* and *'THE NAME OF JESUS'* are used interchangeably. In John 3:16 we read *'believeth in HIM'* but in John 3:18, it states *'believed in the NAME OF THE ONLY BEGOTTEN SON OF GOD'.*

"Wherefore God also hath highly exalted him, and given him a NAME which is above every NAME: that at THE NAME OF JESUS every knee should bow, of things in heaven, and things in earth, and things under the earth..." (Phill. 2:9,10).

The Power and Awesomeness of the entire Godhead (who brought the entire universe into existence), is **IN THE NAME OF JESUS.**
*"In the past God spoke to our forefathers through the prophets at many times and in various ways, but in these last days he has spoken to us by his Son,
whom he appointed heir of all things
and through whom he made the universe*

The son is the RADIANCE OF GOD'S GLORY and the EXACT REPRESENTATION of his BEING, sustaining ALL THINGS by HIS POWERFUL WORD. After he had provided PURIFICATION FOR SINS, he sat down at the right hand of the Majesty in heaven. So he became as much superior than the angels as THE NAME HE HAS INHERITED IS SUPERIOR TO THEIRS" (Hebrews 1:1-4, NIV).

When **THE NAME OF JESUS** is used by the child of God, changes must come, 'chains must be unshackled', sick bodies must be healed and demons must flee **IN NAME OF JESUS.**

- Praying, **IN THE NAME OF JESUS,** for the things He already said he would do, is agreeing with His Word. Where you read 'faith **IN THE NAME OF JESUS'** in the Bible, it indicates a sense of absoluteness and immediacy; in other words, confident expectation for results Now!
Recall that Peter stated to the lame man at the gate called Beautiful, "*Silver and gold have I none, but such as I have, give I unto thee.* **IN THE NAME OF JESUS CHRIST OF NAZARETH** *rise up and walk*" *(Acts 3:2-6).* The result was instantaneous. Verse 16 in that same chapter refers to this miracle. "*By faith IN THE NAME OF JESUS, this man whom you see and know was made strong. It is* **JESUS' NAME AND THE FAITH THAT COMES THROUGH HIM** *that has given this complete healing to him, as you can all see*" *(Acts 3:16, NIV).*

We need more understanding about the Power behind **THE NAME OF JESUS.**

Fact 1.
The Father works IN THE NAME OF JESUS.
Jesus said you will have limitless power from the Father for whatever you ask in **my NAME** (John 16:23,24).

Fact 2.
Jesus works IN HIS OWN NAME.
For the Glory of His Father, Jesus said He would do what ever was asked in His name (John 14:13,14). He did not say to start struggling, praying and fasting to increase your faith, Jesus simply said *'I WILL DO IT'*.

Fact 3.
There are no conditions for the use of the powerful **NAME OF JESUS** except to believe and be filled; Mark 16:16,17.

Fact 4.
There is no need to seek for 'healing ministries', 'deliverance ministries', etc. The Power to minister is in the believer when he/she prays **IN THE NAME OF JESUS.**

"And these signs SHALL FOLLOW them that believe;
In my NAME SHALL they cast out devils;
they SHALL speak with new tongues;
they SHALL take up serpents;
and if they drink any deadly thing,
it SHALL NOT hurt them;
they shall lay hands on the sick
and they SHALL recover" (Mark 16:16-18).

'**SHALL**' in this text speaks of inevitable unconditional results from a believer praying **IN THE NAME OF JESUS.** 'Follow' in this scripture comes from the Greek word 'parakoloutheo' from 'para' meaning beside and 'koloutheo' meaning 'accompany' or literally 'accompanying side by side'. **That is why in Matthew 1:21,23, we read that the meaning 'Emmanuel' is 'God with us'.**

In other words, the **Power of God** is working while you are praying. In Acts 16:16-18 Paul became so aggravated and troubled with the young woman who had a 'demon spirit of divination' that Paul stated "*I command thee IN THE NAME OF JESUS CHRIST to come out of her. And he* (the demon of divination) *came out of her that same hour"*. The simple reality is that as you pray **IN THE NAME OF JESUS, the Power of God WORKS!!!**

- **The method of praying IN THE NAME OF JESUS.**

- We approach the throne of God by praying to the Father **IN THE NAME OF JESUS** because the Father, by sending His Son Jesus, made it possible for us to come before the throne of God.

- We pray **IN THE NAME OF JESUS** because:
1. He is our Saviour; John 3:16.
2. He is our High Priest and Intercessor; Hebrews 4:16.
3. He is our Advocate with the Father; I John 2:1.
4. He is our Healer; Isaiah 53:5, Matthew 8:17, I Peter 2:24.

There are times however that we truly do not know how to pray, but calling the **NAME, JESUS, JESUS, JESUS** is a prayer of completeness. (The founding father of the Church of God in Christ, Charles Harrison Mason, through whom God worked many miracles through, could kneel in prayer for a long as two hours straight saying nothing but **JESUS, JESUS, JESUS, JESUS, JESUS.**)[28]

- First of all, the scripture tells us he that CALLS on the name of Jesus shall be saved (Romans 10:17).
- Secondly, in Jeremiah, the Lord give word for restoration for many desolations of Jerusalem, just *"Call unto me and I will answer thee, and shew thee great and mighty things, which thou knowest not" (Jeremiah 33:3).*

---

[28] Personal communication from my father, Ralph N. Ellis, Sr., who lived in Memphis and attended the Church pastored by Charles Harrison Mason in Memphis, Tennessee from 1922 -1936.

Since all the fullness of the Godhead is invested in **THE NAME OF JESUS**, it seems reasonable to just call the **NAME, JESUS** (especially when problems are so multiple and complex that verbalizing them is difficult).

- Thirdly, the many other names of Jesus are largely descriptive of his awesome power like **'WONDERFUL', 'COUNSELLOR', 'MIGHTY GOD', 'PRINCE OF PEACE'** (Isaiah 9:6). Therefore, calling Jesus is calling all the strength, power and ability that is depicted in his descriptive names.[29]

WEAPONS AGAINST THE ENEMEY: PRAYER AND INTERCESSION

PRAYER and INTERCESSION are Weapons against the Enemy!

> *"And whatsoever ye shall ask in prayer, believing, ye shall receive"* (Matt.21:22)

Prayer is verbal or unspoken communication and communion with the Father, God, **in the Name of His Son, Jesus.** The prayers of the saints is a language that God loves.

> *"And when he had taken the book, the four beasts and four and twenty elders fell down before The Lamb, having every one of them harps <u>**and golden vials full of odours**</u> which are <u>**the prayers of the saints**</u>"* (Rev. 5:8).

God can speak to you in many ways; through the preached word, testimonies, songs and music, or even through nature. God can minister to you because of the intercession of someone else, or with the 'laying on of hands'. However,

---

[29] See APPENDIX IV for the a few of the many descriptive Names of Jesus.

the only way to communicate with God, to tell him your deepest thoughts, your most troublesome fears, your worst hurts, and your greatest needs, is for **YOU TO PRAY** for yourself. **No one can talk to God for you like you can for yourself.**

The **prayers of the saints** are a sweet savour, a wholesome aroma to God and they minister to God. Consequently, through the **prayers of the saints, the God of the universe, of the possible and impossible will work the impossible through your prayers.**

For example...

1. **Paul and Silas,** in spite of severe whipping, sang and **prayed** at midnight. The scripture does not say they **prayed** for an earthquake or even that they travailed for freedom. The Word states simply, **'they sang and prayed at midnight'** and God sent AN EARTHQUAKE which shook the foundations of the prison and the doors were opened, hence their freedom (Acts 16:25,26).

2. **Hezekiah** was sick unto death. He 'turned his face to the wall' and **prayed** and received two miracles. God healed him and extended his life 15 more years plus gave him an UNNATURAL SIGN. God made the earth revolve in reverse, 10 degrees backwards (II Kings 20:11).

3. **Peter** was in prison. The saints **prayed for him without ceasing.** The Word does not indicate how long they **prayed** but **prayer** continued for him as long as he was imprisoned. Because of the prayers of the saints, God sent an angel to lead Peter out of prison (Acts 12:5-10).

4. **God will alter nature.**
"*And another angel came and stood at the altar, having a golden censer; and there was given unto him much incense, that he should offer it with the **prayers of ALL the saints** upon the golden altar which was before the throne. And the smoke of the incense, which came with **the prayers of the saints**, ascended up before God out of the angel's hand. And the angel took the censer, and filled it with fire of the altar, and cast it into the earth: and there were voices, and THUNDERINGS AND LIGHTNINGS AND AN EARTHQUAKE*" *(Revelation 8:3-5).*

It is natural for God to do the unnatural when the saints do what is natural -- **PRAY**. Moreover, **the impossible is mastered when fasting is combined with prayer.** Ninevah, a pagan city, which deserved destruction, changed the heart and intention of God when they repented, **fasted and prayed 3 days and nights** (Jonah).

Jehoshaphat with the tribe of Judah were greatly outnumbered by three enemy nations. However, God caused the enemy nations to ambush and destroy each other because God gave Jehoshaphat and Judah directions for victory after they sought the Lord in fasting and prayer.

It is no wonder that over and over, the Bible encourages the saints to *'pray without ceasing' (II Thess.5:17)*, *'watch and pray' (Matt. 26:41*, *'pray always with all prayer' (Eph. 6:18), etc.* It is the saints greatest privilege to come into the presence of God at anytime (Heb. 4:16) and get a hearing (Psalm 100:3). The saints must cultivate the custom of talking with (and not always to) God, by being in His presence and quietly listening to the voice of God.

Notice that the saints **prayers are answered if:**
1. **We ask according to His Will:**
"*And this is the confidence that we have in him, that, if we ask **anything** according to his will, he heareth us: and*

if we know that he hear us, <u>whatsoever we ask, we know that we have the petitions that we desired of him</u>" (I John 5:14,15).

2. **We are faithful:**
   *"And whatsoever we ask, we receive of him, because, **we keep his commandments** and **do those things which are pleasing in his sight**" (I John 3:22).*

3. **We witness:**
   *"Ye have not chosen me, but I have chosen you and ordained you that ye should go and bring forth fruit, and that your fruit should remain: that **whatsoever ye shall ask the Father in My Name**, he may give it you (John 15:16).*

4. **The Word of Christ abide in you richly (Col. 3:16):**
   *"If ye abide in me, and my words abide in you, **ye shall ask what ye will, and it shall be done unto you**" (John 15:7)*

5. **We tithe** (Malachi 3:10).

Even when we do all the above, God responds according to the consistency of our **prayer life** and the intensity. James (5:16) wrote the 'effectual fervent prayers of a righteous man availeth much' **Effectual fervent prayer** is 'shutting out' the 'cares of this world' and seeking God with all your heart (Jer.29:11-13); and with all types of **praying** (Eph. 6:18; I Tim. 2:1). Moreover, we cannot take our relationship with Christ, nor our position in the Body of Christ, for granted. We need to remember Daniel, who was righteous and greatly beloved; 'he set his face' or became focused entirely on God and began to **seek the Lord with prayer, supplications, with fasting and great humility** (sackcloth and ashes). Further, he repented (even though he was righteous) for himself and Judah.

Note that **YOU ARE AS POWERFUL AS YOUR PRAYER LIFE.**

MUCH PRAYER -- MUCH POWER

Little Prayer -- Little Power

no prayer -- no power[30]

It should be obvious then, why satan works so hard at preventing the saints from **developing a prayer life**. The one thing that counts most with God, it seems the saints do least. In our daily lives we may work 8 hours; sleep 7 hours; eat 2 hours; dress and groom ourselves, 1 hour; travel, 2 hours; leisure time activities (television, telephone, talking, reading, etc.), 3 1/2 hours. Maybe, God gets 1/2 hour of prayer and reading the Word from most Christians. When Christians do manage to get to church, most of the time, once a week, not a great deal of time is spent in prayer.

   Opening prayer: 10 minutes.
   Scripture reading: 5 minutes.
   Devotionals/Choir: 30 minutes.
   Various Offerings: 30 minutes.
   Sermon: 45 minutes.
 Invitation and prayer: 15 Minutes.
   Announcements: 15 Minutes.

Often, the prayer is a type of 'ritualistic cheering squad' prayer during which the congregation energetically repeats every phrase of the prayer leader. Nothing of course is wrong with this, if the Holy Ghost has anointed the prayer leader to pray in this manner. But when the church's and the individual's prayer life is limited to this, there can be no fullness and power in the church or in the individual.

---

[30] Quote of Wigglesworth Smith, a great evangelist in 19th century England.

The founding father of the Church of God in Christ, Charles Harrison Mason, taught **'concert prayer'**, i.e., **everybody pray at the same time.**

How much time is spent in **supplications, prayers, intercessions and giving of thanks** (I Tim. 2:1)? If satan can manage to keep most of the saints from serious travailing **prayer** (and he often does), the church will be in trouble. **A 'prayerless' church is a powerless church; a powerless church is a troubled church.**

Again,

MUCH PRAYER -- MUCH POWER

Little Prayer -- Little Power

no prayer -- no power

Notice, the less one prays, the more difficult it is to pray. The more difficult it is to pray, obviously, the more difficult it is to hear from God. Further, it is unlikely that there will be many 'fillings' (with the Holy Spirit) with a sparse prayer life. Furthermore, the empty saint is in danger of satan's fiery darts because he is void of the 'shield of faith; faith is built up by **PRAYING IN THE HOLY SPIRIT** (Jude 20), as well as by hearing the Word of God (Romans 10:17).

Prayers are unanswered because...
1. Hidden or ignored sin (Psalm 66:18).
2. Refusal to humble oneself, refusal to stop sinning (II Chronicles 7:14).
3. Refusal to hear and accept the Word (Proverbs 28:9).
4. The 'spirit of unforgiveness' (Matthews 6:15).
5. Selfishness, refusal to help the poor (Proverbs 21:13).
6. Self-righteousness (Luke 18:10-14).
7. Vain repetition and entertaining prayers (Matt. 6:5,7).
8. Petitioning for the wrong reasons (James 4:3).

Nevertheless, the Lord, in His omniscience and divine mercy, taught us **how to pray** in such a way that all of our sin, weights, and failures could be dealt with (if we patterned our praying after 'THE LORD'S PRAYER'):

Step 1.
"Our Father which are in heaven, hallowed would be thy name". The word 'hallowed' comes from the same root word as 'hallelujah' which means 'praise the Lord'. We ought to begin all our **prayers** with praise because God likes what He hears when we praise Him. He, then, will enter our **praises** (Ps. 22:3).

Step 2.
"Thy kingdom come". Thy kingdom come refers, in this text, to the time when the Lord returns with his reward. We **pray** 'thy kingdom come' because we know that all the earth is in rebellion against God; only those who have surrendered to the King are eligible for the kingdom. We willingly seek the Lord's return as we prepare for his return. However as we **pray** for his return we must also **pray** 'thy kingdom come'[31] (now in the earth) in the sense of Romans 14:17 which states 'kingdom of God is righteousness, joy and peace in the Holy Ghost'.

Step 3.
"Thy will be done on earth as it in heaven". Submission and obedience is a form of Worship. We reverence the Lord so much that **we put his will before our wants.**

Step 4.
"Give us this day our daily bread". Only then do we begin to **petition** God for personal necessities as well as the needs of others. Notice the 'our' in "our daily bread". Remember,

---

[31] Read Matthew 13 for an description the earthly 'kingdom of God'.

YOU DO NOT HAVE TO SEEK GOD FOR FRINGE BENEFITS. They come subsequent to first **seeking** the kingdom of heaven and all its righteousness (Matthews 6:33) and delighting yourself in pleasing the Lord (Psalm 37:4; Psalm 84:11).

Step 5.
"Forgive us the wrong we have done" (New American Version). We are not perfect even as we strive for perfection. Therefore, lest we sin and offend the Lord in deeds, conversation, thoughts and/or actions, we must repent everyday.

Step 6.
"As we forgive those who have wronged us" (New American Version). If we are really saved and satan is 'the prince of this world', 'offenses' or 'hurts' must come (Luke 17:1). God will not violate his own laws of mercy and forgive you for all you have done when you refuse to forgive someone.

Step 7.
"Lead us not into temptation, but deliver us from evil". God obviously does not lead anyone into temptation. But our prayer must be, 'Lord as we allow you to lead us, help us to know the enemy of our souls'.

Step 8.
"For thine is the kingdom, the power and the glory, forever, Amen". We must end our prayers with praise and worship. For praise tells the Lord that you are satisfied and happy because you have committed everything into his hands. Praise is faith and increases faith.[32]

---

[32] See APPENDIX V for a somewhat different analysis of THE LORD'S PRAYER.

"O God, thou art my God; early will I seek thee: my soul thirsteth for thee, my flesh longeth for thee in a dry and thirsty land, where no water is: To see thy power and thy glory, so as I have seen thee in the sanctuary. When I remember thee upon my bed, and meditate on thee in the night watches. My soul followeth hard after thee" (Ps. 63:1,2,6,8).

PRAYER is 'seeking' (Isaiah 26:9; 55:6).
PRAYER is 'petition (Isaiah 65:24; Matthew 21:22).
PRAYER is 'supplication' (Daniel 9:3-20; Ephesiana 6:18).
PRAYER is 'confession' (Daniel 9:3-20; I John 1:9).
PRAYER is 'thanksgiving' (Phillipians 4:6; I Thess. 5:18).
PRAYER is 'praise' and 'worship' (Psalms 29:1-4,9; 33:1; Daniel 4:34,5).
PRAYER is 'intercession' (Exodus 32:10-14; James 5:14,15).

"He who does not pray; therefore, robs himself of God's help and places God where he cannot help man" *(E.M.Bounds).*

Since **prayer** is a way of concentrating the mind and assembling all the resources of the human personality and spirit for **communion and communication with God**, the physical position when praying may vary.

- Standing, Nehemiah 9:2,3.
- Kneeling, Ezra 9:5.
- Sitting, I Chronicles 17:16-27.
- Bowing, Exodus 34:8.
- Hands uplifted, I Timothy 2:8.

The person who appreciates the **power of prayer**, who has learned **the necessity of prayer**, and who finds **joy in praying**, automatically becomes an **intercessor**. It would follow that **a righteous person who is effectual and fervent in prayer must be an intercessor.**

Intercession means 'the act of making petitions on the behalf of a person'. The **intercessor** must be qualified in order to have the petitions acknowledged and answered. *"If ye abide in me, and my words abide in you, ye shall ask what ye will, and it shall be done unto you" (John 15:7)* indicates that all who are saved have the precondition to intercede on the behalf of others.

Prayer for many Christians becomes a chore that must be performed at designated times. During these episodic **prayer** times, most of us, rarely cry out to God for dying humanity, suffering servants, or for persons not in our family, personal or church network.*"And there is none that calleth upon thy name, that stirreth up himself to take hold of thee: for thou hast hid thy face from us and hast consumed us, because of our iniquities" (Isaiah 64:7).*

Often we in the church complain about rampant crime, rebellious children, spiritually dead churches, dysfunctional families, but we do not 'stand in the gap', grasp a problem and **travail in prayer until God answers**. One of the best descriptions of **intercession** was written by Andrew Murray.

> *"...There are various elements. Of these the chief are perseverance, determination, intensity. It begins with the refusal to at once accept a denial. It grows to the determination to persevere, to spare no time or trouble, till an answer comes. It rises to the intensity in which the whole being is given to God in supplication, and the boldness comes to lay hold of God's strength. At one time it is quiet and restful; at another passionate and bold. Now it takes time and is patient: then again it claims at once what it desires. In whatever different shape, it always means and knows -- God hears prayer: I must be heard"*.[33]

---

[33] The Ministry of Intercession, by Andrew Murray, p 43.

And just like Daniel prayed for 21 days without an answer, but continued in **prayer anyhow, we must pray and intercede** even when it appears the answer is not coming. God promised to answer when we ask according to his will (I John 5:14,15). Even when certain destruction seems imminent, intercessors of God can change the mind of God. The wrath and judgement of God on Israel was stopped because Moses 'stood in the gap' (Exodus 32:9-14). Power and anointing will increase souls will be added when we make the matter of intercession one of our primary focuses in our prayer life.

Behold, I am the Lord God of all flesh: is there anything too hard for me?" (Jer. 32:27).

"Praying always with all prayer and supplication in the Spirit, and watching thereunto with all perseverance and supplication for all saints" (Eph 6:18)

Whenever, THE HOLY GHOST FILLED believer begins praying, he/she is immediately 'warring in the spirit'. We must not only 'pray without ceasing', 'watch and pray' and 'give thanks for all things' to keep the enemy at bay, but also ask God to show us satan's conspiracies and strategies before they are manifested. As the Lord helps us to discern the coming attacks of satan, the Holy Spirit will direct our prayers against the specific strategies and plans of satan.

WEAPONS AGAINST THE ENEMY: PRAISE AND WORSHIP

PRAISE and WORSHIP are WEAPONS against the Enemy!

By Definition, the difference between **praise and worship** is that only the saints can worship, but everyone can **praise**

The Lord. **Praise**, then is defined as a means to extol, laud, honor and acclaim. **Praise** may take numerous forms.

1. Singing, Psalms 57:9; 96:1; 98:1; 100:2.
2. Clapping, Psalm 47:1.
3. Shouting, Psalm 47:1; I Chronicles 15:28.
4. Playing instruments, Psalms 150.
5. Dancing, II Sam.6:14-16; Psalms 149:3; 150:4.
6. Leaping, Acts 3:8.

The method and manner of **praise** may be determined by your personality and your church culture. God will accept extremely divergent acts and utterances of praise. However, one warning about **praise** from God himself: *"I am the Lord,; that is my name and my glory will I not give to another, neither my praise to graven images" (Isaiah 42:8).*

PRAISE is a source of spiritual strength (Nehemiah 8:10) because God dwells in the **praises** of his people (Psalm 22:3). *"Therefore with joy shall ye draw water out of the wells of salvation (Isaiah 12:3).*

Once you enter into the 'gates of the Lord' with **thanksgiving** (just **thanking Him** for another, day, for life, for being able to see, walk and talk, for salvation, etc.) you then move into the 'courts of the Lord' with the **high praises of God** (Ps. 100:3). When you give God the **HIGH PRAISES (WORSHIP), YOU ARE PRAISING HIM FOR WHO HE IS; NOT JUST FOR WHAT HE HAS DONE FOR YOU.** When God is ministered to by you and is pleased with what he hears from you; you have an audience with God.

When your trial is greatest, **PRAISE GOD** (James 1:2,3).

"Wherein ye greatly rejoice, though now for a season, if need be, ye are in heaviness through manifold temptations: That the trial of your faith being much

more precious than of gold that perisheth, though it be tried with fire, might be found unto praise and honour and glory at the appearing of Jesus Christ (I Pe. 1:6,7).

Consider Jehoshaphat and the children of Judah who were surrounded and greatly outnumbered by the Ammonites, Moabites and Edomites. Jehoshaphat fasted and sought the Lord. The Lord assured him not to worry. Jehoshaphat, knowing that God was sovereign and that his Word never failed, called the children of Judah together to instruct them.

"And when he had consulted with the people, he appointed singers unto the Lord, and that should praise the beauty of holiness, as they went out before the army to say, **PRAISE THE LORD,** *for his mercy endureth forever. And when they began to sing and to praise, the Lord set ambushments against the children of Ammon, Moab, and mount Seir which were come against Judah; and they were smitten (II Chronicles 20:21,22).*

Therefore, praising God for everything includes **PRAISING HIM** in adversity. Offering the **'sacrifice of praise'** (Hebrews 13:15) suggests that **praise** is appropriate even when your situation is so difficult, it seems hard to do anything (especially praising God).

PRAISE, then is based on the total and joyful acceptance of the present as a part of God's will (Ephesians 5:20; I Thessalonians 5:18). When you realize the awesome power of your Father, regardless of the trial, you are full of **praise. Praises and joy** in the time of trials demonstrate faith which is pleasing to God. Therefore God acts on your behalf. **Praise** is therefore a weapon against your enemy, satan.

God's word is immutable. It does not matter what satan sends against you, God's word promises, *"No weapon that is formed against thee shall prosper" (Is. 54:17).* The word "prosper" suggests a continuum or process.

Remember, whatever satan sends can't last!
1. Even the hairs on your head are numbered by God (Matthew 10:30).
2. God knows your every thought and the intents of your heart (Psalm 139:1-4).
3. He said he would never leave thee, or forsake thee (Hebrews 13:5).
4. He said he would deliver thee in six troubles; and in seven no evil would touch thee (Job 5:19).
5. He even has given you all the rights of sonship and made you a joint-heir with Christ and an heir of God (John 1:12; Romans 8:17).

PRAISE in its truest sense is **worship**. **Worship is praising God for who He is and not merely for what He has done.** Worship is to acknowledge His **EXCELLENT GREATNESS, HIS PERFECT HOLINESS, HIS AWESOME POWER, HIS INFINITESIMAL CREATIVITY**, etc. Even though our finite minds cannot really comprehend the entire Person and work of God, we can, however, to some extent, comprehend some of the characteristics of God.

To the extent of our understanding, we must **praise** him because **HE IS...**

OMNIPRESENT: *Whither shall I go from thy Spirit? or whither shall I flee from thy presence: If I ascend up into heaven, thou art there: if I make my bed in hell, behold, thou art there. If I take the wings of the morning, and dwell in the uttermost parts of the sea; Even there shall thy hand lead me, and thy right hand shall hold me..."* (Psalm 139:7-9)

IMMENSE: "*But will God indeed dwell on the earth? behold, the heaven and the heaven of heavens cannot contain thee; how much less this house that I have builded?"* (I Kings 8:27).

SELF-SUFFICIENT: "*And God said unto Moses, I AM THAT I AM: and he said, thus shalt thou say unto the children of*

Israel, **I AM** hath sent me unto you" (Exodus 3:14). "But our God is in the heavens:he hath done whatsoever he hath pleased" (Psalm 115:3).

IMMUTABLE: "For I am the Lord, I change not ..."(Mal. 3:6). "Jesus Christ, the same yesterday, and today and forever" (Heb.13:8).

HOLY: "And one cried to another, and said, Holy, Holy, Holy, is the Lord of Hosts: the whole earth is full of His Glory" (Isaiah 6:3).

EXCELLENT: "Touching the Almighty, we cannot find him out: he is excellent in power, and in judgement, and in plenty of justice..." (Job 37:23).

WISDOM: "O Lord, how manifold are thy works! in wisdom hast thou made them all: the earth is full of thy riches" (Psalm 104:24).

MAJESTY: "The voice of the Lord is over the waters: the God of glory thunders, the Lord thunders over the mighty waters. The voice of the Lord is powerful; the voice of the Lord is majestic" (Psalms 29:3,4 NIV).

CREATIVITY: "For by him all things were created: things in heaven and on earth, visible and invisible, whether thrones or powers or rulers or authorities; all things were created by him and for him. He is before all things, and in him all things hold together" (Colossians 1:16,17 NIV).

STEADFAST: "But I will not take my love from him, nor will I ever betray my faithfulness. I will not violate my covenant or alter what my lips have uttered" (Psalm 89:33,34 NIV).

INVINCIBLE: *"Ah Lord God! behold, thou hast made the heaven and tthe earth by thy great power and stretched out arm, and there is nothing too hard for thee..." (Jeremiah 32:17).*

ABLE: *"Now unto him who is able to do immeasurably more than all we ask or imagine, according to his power that is at work within us..." (Ephesians 3:20, NIV).*

WEAPONS AGAINST THE ENEMY: SPEAKING IN AN UNKNOWN TONGUE

SPEAKING IN 'UNKNOWN TONGUES' is a WEAPON against the Enemy!

Briefly, let's review the reasons that **speaking or praying in an unknown tongue** is an individualized weapon against satan. There are times in a Christian's walk with the Lord when the spiritual warfare is so extreme, that praying normally is inadequate. In these times the Holy Ghost will make intercession through you and for you in a heavenly language (Romans 8:26,27; Isaiah 28:11,12). **Satan does not have the gift of interpretation**; he therefore does not know the content of the prayers or praises.
Then you are,
1. In perfect communion and communication with God.
2. We are being edified and refreshed (I Cor. 14:4).

There will be no discussion on the 'gift of tongues' which is multiplicity of heavenly languages and/or the multiplicity of earthly languages which have not been learned by the speaker --'other tongues'; nor of tongues that flow which must be followed by interpretation (I Corinthians 12:10; Acts 2:7-11).
Tongues are heavenly languages given by the Holy Ghost as a sign to the unbeliever (I Corinthians 14:22 and a sign of the believer (Mark 16:17).

SELF-EXAMINATION
THE WEAPONS AGAINST THE ENEMY

1. Have you been Baptized and Filled with the Holy Ghost?

2. Have you been refilled with the Holy Ghost lately?

3. Do you know why you 'plead THE BLOOD OF JESUS?

4. Can you explain to a 'baby' saint the Power in THE BLOOD OF JESUS?

5. Do you know why you have the AUTHORITY to use THE NAME OF JESUS.

6. Can you explain to someone why you pray to the Father IN THE NAME OF JESUS?

7. Do you know where the scriptures are found that assures you of the Power of God in you?

8. Can you find scriptures pertaining to forgiveness and salvation without using your concordance?

9. Do you know why you praise God?

10. Can you explain why only the saints can worship God?

11. When you 'speak in tongues', do you feel refreshed?

12. When you 'speak in tongues', are you sure the Holy Ghost gave you the utterance?

HOW TO KNOW THE WILL OF GOD FOR MY LIFE

The Greatness of God can be yours!!!

The Greatness of God should be yours!!!

The Greatness of God will be yours !!!

The Greatness of God is yours!!!

God has a special 'blueprint' for every person, which He gradually reveals and brings to pass as the person continues to surrender and seek God. A 'blueprint' is God's special, glorious, perfect plan for every person's life. His plan for each person is based on the individual's abilities, personality and absolute obedience to God -- total submission. Sad as it is, most will never find that glorious perfect plan.

> *"And the cares of this world, and the deceitfulness of riches and the lusts of other things ENTERING IN, choke the word, and it becometh unfruitful"* (Mark 4:19).

What are these some of things that hinder, stop and block the PERFECT WILL OF GOD in our lives?
1. 'The cares of this world':
   - Broken heart.
   - Rebellious children
   - Dependent and sick relatives.

- Unpaid bills.[34]
- Sickness.
- Homelessness.
2. 'The deceitfulness of riches':
   - Money is power for me.
   - Fabulous clothes and cars make the man.
   - Money can buy any position.
3. 'The lusts of other things':
   - For Fame.
   - For riches.
   - For acceptance in elite circles.
   - For the 'right' neighborhood.

How many people (not gifted persons who can emotionally and intellectually stimulate you), do you know that manifest the Glory or Greatness of God in their lives?

> "*And be not conformed to this world: but be ye <u>TRANSFORMED</u> by the renewing of your mind that ye may <u>PROVE</u>, WHAT IS THAT <u>good</u>, and <u>acceptable</u>, and <u>PERFECT WILL OF GOD</u> (Romans 12:2).*

The concept of 'living sacrifice' is simply obedient consistent service; not serving God when it is comfortable or convenient, but with a commitment to please God, regardless of personal circumstances or feeling.

'Be not conformed to this world' -- You must divorce yourself from the innate characteristics of this world system; greed, evil and corruption.

'Be ye transformed' -- This word 'transformed' is the same word that is used in the transfiguration narratives about Jesus (Matthew 17:2 Mark 9:2-8). However, for the believer, it is a spiritual process, and not a single event because of the...

---

[34] See **AFFLICTIONS, WHY ME?** by Dr. Fay Ellis Butler

'**Renewing of your mind**' in prayer (Phillipians 4:6,7) and in the Word (Psalm 119:1,11).

'**That ye may prove**', or show or demonstrate truth;

'**What is that good**', that which leads to spiritual and moral growth as a Christian;

'**And acceptable**' that which is pleasing to God;

'**And perfect WILL OF GOD**', that which completely satisfies God -- your unconditional obedience.

SPECIFICALLY, HOW DOES THE SAINT <u>PROVE</u> WHAT IS THAT <u>GOOD</u> AND <u>ACCEPTABLE</u> WILL OF GOD?

How often do you hear people testify: "I know that the Lord has something for me to do but I do not know what it is"? Or, worse yet, how often do you observe individuals attempting to preach like someone else, or minister like some one else or even pretend to demonstrate the Power of God (phony prophesying, phony tongues, phony quickening)?

'**Proving what is that good and acceptable will of God**' is simply knowing the Word, and abiding in the Word. In other words, knowing that ...

- The WILL OF GOD for every Christian is his/her sanctification (I Thessalonians 4:3).
- The WILL OF GOD for every Christian is giving thanks for <u>everything</u> (I Thessalonians 5:18).
- The WILL OF GOD for every Christian is doing good (I Peter 2:15).
- The WILL OF GOD for every Christian <u>includes</u> suffering for doing the right thing (I Peter 3:17).

Instead of worrying about some special area or gift as the **WILL OF GOD**, why not start with the basics. Ask yourself is God pleased with my faithfulness, my service to Him and my seeking (Haggai 1:4-7).

"I delight to do thy Will of my God: Yea thy law is

within my Heart" (Psalm 40:8).

For example,
1. Do you go to church at least one night per week at the beginning of prayer and pray 'through'? (ITimothy 2:1).
2. Do you pay your tithes like you earn them? (Malachi 3:10).
3. Do you attend at least one of your church's Bible training sessions per week; e.g. Sunday School, or Bible Study? (II Timothy 2:15).
4. Have you begun to get a personal command of the scriptures?
   - Do you know at least one victory scripture? For example, I John 4:4.
   - Do You know at least one survival scripture? For example, Hebrews 13:5.
   - Do you know at least one confidence building scripture? For example, Phillipians 4:12,13.
   - Do you know scriptures to strengthen your will? For example, Phillipians 4:8.
   - Do you know satan-defeating scriptures? For example, Luke 10:19.
   - Do you know praise scriptures? For example, Exodus 15:2.
5. Do you witness to at least one person per week who does not belong to your church? Acts 1:8.
6. Do you keep your fast days, even if you only make it until noon? Do you go on the consecrations as the pastor call them? (You should have at least one time of special consecration a year.)
7. If you believe you have been anointed or appointed to a special work with or over God's people, do you spend extra time in prayer, fasting and in the Word seeking direction?
8. Are you involved in at least one outreach ministry? Jeremiah 8:20, Matthew 9:37,38. For example,
   - The tract ministry,

- Child evangelism,
- Street ministry,
- Prison ministry,
- Telephone reassurance,
- Door-to-door witnessing,
- Hospital/Visiting the Sick and Shut-in.

9. Do you, from time to time, financially assist some needy person in your congregation without waiting for a specific person at church or special organization/club to do it? Matthew 25:38,39.
10. Even if you do not have a 'hospital ministry', when you do visit hospitalized friends or relatives, do you stop to give a hospitalized person, unknown to you, a word of encouragement? Matthew 25:29.
11. In almost every congregation, there are senior citizens that could use some assistance from time to time. Do you assist those who need help? Galatians 6:10.[35]

In other words, if you are going 'to prove life what is that good and acceptable WILL OF GOD', you are going to start working without someone having to direct you and you will keep working (even when no one acknowledges your labor).

> *"Whatsoever thy hand findeth to do, do it with thy might; for there is no work, nor device, nor knowledge, nor wisdom, in the grave, whither thou goest" (Ecclesiastes 9:10).*

You are going to work for the right reasons: *"Not with eyeservice, as menpleasers; but as the servants of Christ, doing the WILL OF GOD from the heart" (Ephesians 6:6).*

You are working in order that the Holy Ghost have free course to work in you. The tragedy for the saints is that life is soon 'past and gone', and most of the 'works' done have

---

[35] See Appendix VI for a more detailed Self-Evaluation.

been done for self-serving reasons. Preaching to please (or to be praised), singing to be seen, presiding to be powerful, will be tried in fire; these kinds of 'works' will be burned as hay and stubble (I Corinthians 3:13,14).

HOW DOES THE HOLY GHOST BRING ABOUT THE PERFECT WILL OF GOD IN MY LIFE?

You must allow the Holy Ghost to work in your life (See Acts 7:51; Ephesians. 4:30). *"For as many are led by the Spirit of God, they are the sons of God" (Romans 8:14).* The mechanics of being *'being led by the Spirit of God'* are a mystery. However, in the Christian, whose ears and heart are 'open' with the Holy Ghost, abiding (dwelling) in your sanctified Blood Washed human spirit, will...

- Guide you by speaking directly to you through your spirit, or through someone else who is directed by the Holy Ghost (John 16:13);
- Teach you by direct revelation or discernment, or by those who the God has called and the Holy Ghost has anointed to teach (I Corinthians 2:10-13, John 14:26);.
- Call you to one or more of His ministries or to minister in specific situations (Ephesians 4:11-13, Romans 12:6-8, ,8 I Corinthians 12:28).

Remember, The Holy Spirit cannot work in a vacuum; you must present Him not only your total self, but something to work with, **THE WORD OF GOD** hidden in your heart. Therefore you must, in order to yield and seek, know who, what and why you are yielding and seeking. This can only be ascertained through the Word and prayer. You must study the Word, meditate on the Word, memorize the Word as well as pray.

The Holy Ghost will clearly speak to you about what to say when you are witnessing, how to pray when you are praying, even which area of the ministry you are best suited for and how to develop yourself in ministry.

Elder John Lawrence gave a formula, in his Soul Winning Book, to know when God is speaking to you (since what you are hearing can be <u>God's voice , your own voice or satan's voice</u>). He gave the following four things to do when in doubt:
1. Find the scriptures that agree or disagree with what you are told to do; if none, quote Proverbs 3:6.
2. Always plead the **Blood of Jesus** against any impression or thought you are not sure of; if it is God, the **Blood of Jesus** won't hurt Him. If it is not God, the impression or thought will flee (Revelations 12:11).
3. Ask the Holy Spirit to lift a standard against it (Isaiah 59:19).
4. Resist it if you are not positive that it is God (James 4:7).[36]

When you have done all the above, and it is God talking to you, He will definitely, show you his authority and providence. For example, if he is calling you to 'a ministry of mercy and compassion' (Romans 12:8), you will find your attention always drawn to persons 'hurting' or God will send 'wounded'/'hurting' persons to you -- God's <u>providence</u>. You will find that as soon as you talk with them, maybe hug them and tell them that you understand what they are going through, and/or pray with them, that these persons are lifted and often healed of the hurt -- God's <u>authority</u>.

As you are move in the faith and anointing of God, the Holy Ghost will direct and teach you (I John 2:27). You will find God using your mouth with those things you did not know or that had not occurred to you -- 'Word of Knowledge'.

Finally, when the Holy Ghost leads, instructs and guides, the work, the labor, the deliverance, the healing, etc. endure.

---

[36] See **SOUL WINNER'S INSTITUTE; Training You to work for God**, by **Rev. John D. Lawrence.**

HOW WILL I KNOW THAT I AM IN THE WILL OF GOD?

I   The **FRUIT OF THE SPIRIT** will be recognized because persons who are 'sold out' to God are 'living epistles' (II Corinthians 3:2).

The all of the **FRUIT OF THE SPIRIT** will be easily observed in your life. The FRUIT (singular not plural) is the character of Holy Ghost.
Having been filled with the Holy Ghost, the Christian should represent the character of the Holy Ghost. Granted, some of the aspects of the character of the Holy Ghost may be more observable in individuals than other aspects. For example, 'meekness' may be perfected more in the believer's life than 'goodness'. However, since growth in God and sanctification never cease in the believer, these facets (of the character) of the Holy Ghost will always be increasing in the believer.

THE FRUIT OF THE SPIRIT IS:
Love,
   Joy,
      Peace,
         Longsuffering,
            gentleness,
               goodness,
                  faith,
                     meekness,
                        temperance (Galations 5:22.23).

1. **Love**
The first thing that shows is **love**. This kind of **love** has to do with caring, sharing and giving of oneself, to the extent, that relatives, friends, co-workers, even enemies recognize that this is God's **love**.

*"Dear friends, let us **LOVE** one another, for **LOVE** comes from God. Everyone who **LOVES** has been born of God and knows God. Whoever does not **LOVE** does not know God, because **GOD IS LOVE**. ...Dear friends, since God so **LOVED** us, we also ought to **LOVE** one another. No one has seen God; but if we **LOVE** one another, <u>God lives in us and his love is made complete in us</u> (I John 4:7-12, NIV).*

2. <u>Joy</u>

In this text 'joy' is derived from the Greek word 'chara' meaning delight and gladness. **Joy** as fruit, is a state of being, related to contentment. Contentment derives from the knowledge of fellowship with the Father. This is the same definition for 'joy' from the Hebrew word 'chadah' found in Nehemiah 8:10, "...*the **JOY** of the Lord is your strength*".

3. <u>Peace</u>.

From the Greek word 'eirene' suggesting 'quietness and rest' but in addition, 'harmony in relationships'. When you have surrendered everything to God, you know whatever happens, good or bad, it's all right. God has everything, including you and your circumstances, under His control. Jesus said,

*"Peace I leave with you, my **PEACE** I give unto you: **not as the world giveth, give I unto you**" (John 14:27). "And the **PEACE** of God which passeth all understanding, shall keep your hearts and minds through Christ Jesus (Phillipians 4:7)*

4. <u>Longsuffering</u>

'Makrothumos' is the Greek word from which the meaning of 'longsuffering' comes, suggesting 'forbearance', and 'fortitude'. Fortitude is the strength of mind that allows one to endure pain or adversity with courage. Forbearance is tolerance and patience in the face of provocation. Read the charge to preachers in II Timothy 4:2;

*"...Reprove, rebuke, exhort with all **LONGSUFFERING** and doctrine"*.

5. **Gentleness**.
'Kindness', 'goodness of heart' or 'moral excellence in character or demeanor' from the Greek word 'chrestotes' is the actual meaning behind gentleness

6. **Goodness**.
'Chrestotes' is the also word that gives us the meaning of **'goodness'** but in this sense it indicates **'goodness'** in action and deeds, rather than only as a quality. Paul wrote to the Romans saying,
> "...*That ye also are full of goodness, filled with all knowledge, able also to admonish one another*" (15:14).

7. **Faith**.
From 'pistis', we find these meanings of **'faith'**: a) a firm conviction, producing a full acknowledgement of God's revelation or truth; b) a personal surrender to Him; c) a conduct inspired by such surrender.[37]
> "*We are bound to thank God always for you, brethren, as it is meet, because that your **FAITH** groweth exceedingly, and the charity of every one of you all toward each other aboundeth*" (II Thessalonians 1:3).

8. **Meekness**.
The Greek word 'Prautes' denotes **'meekness'** as an attitude of the soul towards a Mighty God; an humble heart that does not struggle, nor resist, nor contend with God. This attitude also suggest that in the face of insults, abuse and injuries, that **'meekness'** accepts this as the 'chastening of the Lord'.
> "*To speak evil of no man, to be no brawlers, but gentle, shewing all meekness unto all men*" (Titus 3:2).

9. **Temperance.**
'Temperance' translated from the Greek Word 'enkrateia' which is derived from the Greek verb meaning strength. The literal translation is 'self-control'. In other words, the person

---

[37] All definitions from Greek words are extracted from Strong's Concordance and Vine's Expository Dictionary of Bible Words.

in the Will of God will have the strength to control his/her mouth, appetites (eating disorders).

II FRUIT WILL BE HARVESTED if I am in the WILL OF GOD.

It is mandated that each child of God bear or harvest fruit. If you do not sow any seed, you can not expect a harvest. Accordingly, you ought to be able to claim responsibility for influencing at least one person per year to make a decision for Christ.

> *"He that goeth forth and weepeth, bearing precious seed, shall doubtless come again with rejoicing, BRINGING SHEAVES WITH HIM" (Psalm 126:6).*

The PERFECT WILL OF GOD is always in the 'harvest' of the dying and lost souls. Today, the 'harvest' is extensive in our homes, on our jobs and in our communities. For example,

1. Homeless persons are in every city in this country and can be found in most towns. If a person in the street asks you for money, take the opportunity to witness and pray for them if possible.
2. Where crowds congregate, get your tape recorder, a Maximouse (portable amplifier and microphone), play some appropriate Gospel music, and preach the Word. Just take one other person, if the other 'saints' are afraid.
3. Keep tracts in your purse, wallet or car and pass them out when God gives you the opportunity.
4. Take your neighbor's children to Sunday School.

> *"Ye have not chosen me but I have chosen you, and ordained you, that ye should go and <u>BRING FORTH FRUIT</u>, and that your <u>fruit should remain</u>: that whatsoever ye shall ask of the Father in my name, he may give it you (John 15:16).*

III The POWER OF GOD WILL BE MANIFESTED

With every believer who is 'in God' and 'God is in him/her', certain signs will identify, his/her 'sonship'-- the right to use the NAME OF JESUS and to get RESULTS.

"He that believeth and is baptized shall be saved, but he that believeth not shall be damned.And these signs SHALL FOLLOW THEM THAT BELIEVE;
In MY NAME SHALL THEY CAST OUT DEVILS;
THEY SHALL SPEAK WITH NEW TONGUES;
...THEY SHALL LAY HANDS ON THE SICK AND THEY SHALL RECOVER"(Mark 16:16-18).

"I have given you AUTHORITY TO TRAMPLE ON SNAKES AND SCORPIONS and to OVERCOME ALL THE POWER OF THE ENEMY; nothing will harm you (Luke 10:19, NIV).

IV THE MINISTRY OR LABOR WILL ENDURE.

You will know you are in the PERFECT WILL OF GOD when your labor -- souls saved, broken hearts healed, captive minds freed -- continues. It will endure because those ministered to (by you) will begin to minister and witness to others.

"Every man's work shall be made manifest: for the day shall declare it, because it shall be revealed by fire; and the fire shall try every man's work of what sort it is.If any man's work abide which he hath built thereupon, he shall receive a reward" (I Corinthians 3:13,14).

WHEN WILL I KNOW THAT I AM IN THE WILL OF GOD?

At every stage of your walk with God you can be in the PERFECT WILL OF GOD. The perfection that God requires of each us is to live at the level dedication and commitment that we have learned and understand. This means that the 'baby saint' and the Bishop can both be in the 'PERFECT WILL OF GOD'. Both must live according to Word and at the level of his/her comprehension of the Word.

In other words, at every stage of your walk with God, you should be in the Will of God. Although, God does not change (Hebrews 13:8), His will for your life is not 'static'. Look at Phillip:
- He was first a follower or a disciple (John 1:43-49).
- He was a seeker, seeking to be filled with the Holy Ghost (Acts 1:13).
- He was a deacon, ministering to material and spiritual needs of the church (Acts 6:1-5).
- He was a great evangelist 'turning the world upside down' (Acts 8:5-13; 21:8; 8:26-40).

Further when you have truly sold out to God...
1. **You will never feel worthy:**
   "Whereof I was made a minister, according to the gift of the Grace of God given unto me by the effectual working of his power. Unto me, <u>WHO AM LESS THAN THE LEAST OF ALL SAINTS</u>, is this Grace given, that I should preach among the Gentiles the unsearchable riches of Christ" (Eph 3:7,8; cf Phillipians 2:3,4).

Arrogant, haughty persons demanding and commanding recognition, attention, power, position and 'a chance to put on a performance with singing, teaching or preaching' are not in the WILL OF GOD.

2. **You will never cease from seeking:**
   "I want to know Christ and the power of his resurrection and the fellowship of sharing in his sufferings, becoming like him in death, and so, somehow to attain to the resurrection from the dead. Not that I have already

obtained all this, or <u>have already been made perfect</u>, but I press on to take hold of that which Christ Jesus took hold of me.Brothers, I do not consider myself yet to have taken hold of it.But one thing I do: Forgetting what is behind and straining toward what is ahead,
I PRESS
ON TOWARD THE GOAL TO WIN THE PRIZE for which God called me heavenward in Christ Jesus" (Phillipians 3:10-14, NIV; see also Psalm 63:1,2).

3. **You will always be ready to work for God:**
   "So, as much as in me is, I am ready to preach the gospel to you that are in Rome also.For I am not ashamed of the Gospel of Christ: for it is the power of God unto salvation to every one that believeth; to the Jew first, and also to the Greek. For therein is <u>the righteousness of God revealed</u> from faith to faith..." (Romans 1:15-17).

   "But truly I am full of power by the spirit of the Lord, and of judgment, and of might to declare unto Jacob his transgression, and to Israel his sin" (Micah 3:8).

The best conclusion to the whole idea of being in the Lord's PERFECT WILL is what God himself stated:

> ***"Thus saith the Lord, Let not the wise man glory in his wisdom, neither let the mighty man glory in his might, let not the rich man glory in his riches:But let him that glorieth glory in this, that he <u>UNDERSTANDETH</u> and <u>KNOWETH ME</u>, that I am the Lord which exercise lovingkindness, judgment and righteousness in the earth: for in these things I delight, saith the Lord" (Jer. 9:23,24).***

CONCLUSION

*"And now brethren (and sisters), **I commend you to God and to the word of his Grace, WHICH IS ABLE TO BUILD YOU UP**, and give you an inheritance among all them which are sanctified" (Acts 20:32).*

There are no 'little yous' and 'BIG MEs' in the family of God; we are members of the same Body and that Body, Jesus Christ, is the Church. A "new" saint is just as saved as an "old" saint. Moreover, as soon as you are saved, you are an 'ambassador for Christ'(II Corinthians 5:17-20).

Experience and knowledge (studying the Word, witnessing, praying, fasting and continuously humbling oneself) prepares the saint to be elevated in God. However, the Holy Spirit and the ministry is invested in everyone who is saved (I Corinthians 12:11)

The ministry can include;[38]

1. Apostles, prophets, evangelists, pastors and teachers (Ephesians 4:11).
2. Prophecy, ministry (service of a deacon), teaching, exhortation, giving, ruling, mercy (Romans 12:6-8).
3. The Word of Wisdom, the Word of Knowledge, faith, gifts of healing, the working of miracles, prophecy, discerning of spirits, divers kinds of tongues, and interpretation of tongues (I Corinthians 12:8-10).
4. Helps, governments (I Corinthians 12:28).

Just as God gives the Gift of the Holy Ghost to those who obey Him (Acts 5:32), He likewise grants special ministries to

---

[38] There are many ministries of the Holy Ghost for the Body of Christ. Not all are written in the Bible; for example, counseling, peacemaking, etc.

those He can trust and who also will not take any of His Glory for themselves. If indeed you are called and anointed with ministry, are you 'waiting' for further spiritual development by...
- Fasting and praying consistently.
- Studying the Word of God, particularly those scriptures that pertain to your ministry.
- By doing whatever your hands find to do.
- By witnessing.
- By being faithful to your church, pastor and to the stewardship of your finances (tithes and offering).

IT IS IMPOSSIBLE TO BY-PASS THE BASICS TO GREATNESS.

Before God will endow and invest you with special ministries, God has to know that he can trust you, that you are a clean vessel, and that you will move with the Spirit when He orders you to move. As you continue to perfect yourself and 'decrease', the Holy Ghost and ministries will 'increase', Your prayers, fasting, faithfulness and obedience energize God to work for and through you.

Remember, if you cannot seek out the backslider and/or witness to the sinner whom you know, it is unlikely and improbable that God is going to empower or anoint your to preach, prophecy, heal and deliver those unknown to you.

Furthermore, **a person who calls himself a preacher, evangelist, apostle, healer or prophet, is not necessarily a preacher, evangelist, apostle, healer, or prophet that God has called or sent.** God confirms Himself in the ministries of His servants with results. **Emotionalism is not necessarily a work of God.**

IT IS IMPOSSIBLE TO BY-PASS THE BASICS TO GREATNESS.

Are you ready to move on God's terms? Remember God

may call on you to do the unusual. Study the life and times of God's servants in the Bible.

- In order to emphasize the message of God to Egypt and Ethiopia, Isaiah walked naked and barefoot three years (Is. 20:2,3).
- In order to carry message and 'hurt' of God more effectively about the whoredom of Israel and Judah, Hosea by God's commandment married Gomer, a whore (Hosea 1:2).
- Ezekiel shaved all the hair from his head and face (which was very unusual in those times) to prophetically utter and demonstrate the destruction of his people. One third of his hair he burned, one third was 'smitten about' with a knife and the remaining third was scattered to the wind (Eze 5:1-4).

CAN GOD TRUST YOU?
HAVE YOU KEPT YOUR VOWS?
HAVE YOU MASTERED THE BASICS?

Most of us, unfortunately, are not prepared to be elevated in God. We have not passed the first step, that is, we have not brought all the 'fruits worthy of repentance'. Some have long forgotten that sanctification is a daily continuous process. Worse yet, most of us, if we were indeed Baptized with the Holy Ghost, act as though our pursuit or seeking of God was completed. Understand that **The Holy Ghost is our 'passport' to enter the 'Holy of Holies'**, namely, the mysteries and greatness of God. In other words, receiving the Baptism of the Holy Ghost is only the beginning.

God is looking for a man, woman, boy or girl to 'stand in the gap'. However, you cannot stand unprepared. Unpreparedness invites disaster. God **wants you to prepare yourself so that He can use you.**

YOU ARE 'CALLED TO BE A SAINT'!

ARE YOU AVAILABLE?
HAVE YOU MASTERED THE BASICS?

*"His **DIVINE POWER HAS GIVEN US EVERYTHING WE NEED FOR LIFE AND GODLINESS** through our knowledge of him who <u>CALLED US by his own glory</u> and goodness.*

*Through these **HE HAS GIVEN US HIS VERY GREAT AND PRECIOUS PROMISES**, so that through them you may participate in the divine nature and escape the corruption in the world caused by evil desires.*

For this reason, make every effort to
add to your faith goodness;
and to goodness, knowledge;
and to knowledge, self-control;
and to self-control, perseverance;
and to perseverance, godliness;
and to godliness, brotherly kindness;
and to brotherly kindness, love.
For if you possess these qualities in **INCREASING MEASURE, THEY WILL KEEP YOU FROM BEING INEFFECTIVE AND UNPRODUCTIVE** in your knowledge of our Lord Jesus Christ" (II Peter 1:3-8,NIV).

APPENDIX I
The Tongue's Diversity

The <u>tongue</u> is central to the work of the church. Notice the ministries that will not go on without speech.

PREACHING: Mark 16:15.
TEACHING: Titus 2:1.
COUNSELING: James 5:16.
PROPHESYING: Romans 12:8.
THE WORD OF KNOWLEDGE: I Corinthians 12:8.
THE WORD OF WISDOM: I Corinthians 12:8.
DIVERSITIES OF TONGUES: I Corinthians 12:10.
INTERPRETATION OF TONGUES: I Corinthians 12:10.

Also, the <u>tongue</u> is used to help 'maintain' life:

Correction; II Timothy 3:16.
Rebuke; Titus 1:13.
Encouragement; Romans 12:8.

Notice satan is the supreme imitator and will also use the <u>tongue</u>, but to destroy.

Backbiting; II Corinthians 12:20, cf. Psalms 15:3.
Lying; John 8:44, Psalm 58:3, Proverbs 21:6.
Cursing; Psalm 59:12.
Blaspheming; Daniel 7:25.
Seducing; Proverbs 7:21.
Intrigue; Proverbs 6:13.
Flattering; Proverbs 6:24.
Muttering; Isaiah 59:3.

APPENDIX II
The Complexity of the Heart

The heart is:[39]

1. The seat of physical life, Acts 14:17; James 5:5.

2. The seat of moral nature and spiritual life, the seat of
   - Grief, John 14:1; Romans 9:2; 2 Corinthians 2:4;
   - Joy, John 16:22; Eph 5:19;
   - The desires, Matt. 5:28; 2 Peter 2:14;
   - The perceptions, John 12:40, Ephesians 4:18;
   - The affections, Luke 24;32; Acts 21:13;
   - The thoughts Matthews 9:4; Hebrews 4:12;
   - The understanding, Matthews 13:15; Romans 1:21;
   - The reasoning powers, Mark 2:6; Luke 24:38;
   - The imagination, Luke 1:51;
   - Conscience, Acts 2:37; I John 3:20;
   - The intentions, Hebrews 4:12, compare I Peter 4:1;
   - Purpose, Acts 11:23; 2 Corinthians 9:7;
   - The will; Roman 6:17; Romans 10:10; Hebrews 3:12.

---

[39] **VINE'S EXPOSITORY DICTIONARY OF BIBLE WORDS.**

APPENDIX III
SCRIPTURE MEMORIZATION

You need to plan how you are going to continuously memorize scripture. The basics to any Bible memory plan are as follows.

1. **Develop a system for the areas to be memorized.** For example you should begin with scriptures that give reasons to memorize scripture; Psalm 119:11,105, Col. 3:16. Or, warfare scriptures; Luke 10:19, James 4:7, Matt.16:19, I John 4:4; Rev.12:11. Or, healing scriptures; Isaiah 53:5, Matthew 8:17, I Peter 2:24; Psalms 100:3.

2. **Develop a method.** For Example, take 3'x 5' cards, write on them the scriptures to be memorized. Place them in your bag or briefcase, in the pocket of your car. When you have spare time, take them out and study them. At home place the scripture that you are currently memorizing over the sink in the kitchen, or over the bathroom sink, etc. Review and memorize. Memorize and review.

3. **Whenever you hear a message that is particularly meaningful to you or that does something special for you, take the text of message and memorize it.** These are the easiest scriptures to memorize because the message of is in your heart already.

4. **When satan is tormenting your mind, discipline your mind by learning more scriptures.** Challenge yourself to learn the entire 27th Psalm or the entire 8th chapter of Romans.

5. At the Beginning of weekly Bible study for 15 minutes ask the pastor to allow you to have Bible memory course conducted. It is easier to memorize scripture when you work at it with others.

APPENDIX IV
DESCRIPTIVE NAMES OF JESUS

Advocate,	I John 2:1.
Almighty,	Revelations 19:15.
Alpha and Omega,	Revelations 21:6.
Ancient of Days,	Daniel 7:9.
Apostle of our profession,	Hebrews 3:1.
Author/finisher of our faith	Hebrews 12:2.
Blessed and only Potentate,	I Timothy 6:15.
Bread of Life,	John 6:35.
Chief Corner Stone,	Mark 12:10.
Chief Shepherd,	I Peter 5:4.
Christ, The Power of God,	I Corinthians 1:24.
Counselor,	Isaiah 9:6.
Covenant of the people,	Isaiah 42:6.
Deliverer,	Romans 11:26.
Door,	John 10:2
Everlasting Father,	Isaiah 9:6.
Faithful and True,	Revelations 19:11.
Head over all things,	Ephesians 1:22.
Holy One,	I John 2:20.
Image of the Invisible God,	Colossians 1:15.
Immanuel,	Isaiah 7:14.
King of Glory,	Psalm 24:7.
King of Kings,	I Timothy 6:15.
Lamb of God,	John 1:36.
Lion of the tribe of Judah,	Revelations 5:5.
Morning Star,	Revelations 22:16.
Our Passover,	I Corinthians 5:7.
Resurrection and the Life,	John 11:25.
Shepherd of our souls,	I Peter 2:25.
Sower, Matthew 13,3,37. Door,	John 10:2.
Teacher from God,	John 3:2.
True Vine,	John 15:1.
Truth/Way,	John 14:6.
Word of God,	Revelations 19:13.

APPENDIX V
THE LORD'S PRAYER

I can not say "*OUR*" if I live in a watertight spiritual compartment, if I think a special place in heaven is reserved for my denomination.

I can not say "*FATHER*" if I do not demonstrate the relationship in my daily life.

I can not say "*WHICH ART IN HEAVEN*" if I am so occupied with earth that I am laying up no treasure over there.

I can not say "*HALLOWED BE THY NAME*" if I, who am called by His name, am not Holy.

I can not say "*THY WILL BE DONE*" if I am questioning, resentful, or disobedient to His will for me.

I can not say "*ON EARTH AS IT IS IN HEAVEN*" if I am not prepared to devote my life here to His service.

I can not say "*GIVE US THIS DAY OUR DAILY BREAD*" if I am living on past experiences.

I can not say "*FORGIVE US OUR DEBTS AS WE FORGIVE OUR DEBTORS*" if I harbor a grudge against anyone.

I can not say "*LEAD US NOT INTO TEMPTATION*" if I deliberately place myself or remain in a position where I am likely to be tempted.

I can not say "*DELIVER US FROM EVIL*" if I am not prepared to fight in the spiritual realm with the weapon of prayer.

I can not say "*THINE IS THE KINGDOM*" if I do not give the KING the disciplined obedience of a loyal subject.

I can not say "*THINE IS THE GLORY*" if I am seeking Glory for myself.

I can not say "*FOREVER*" if my horizons are bounded by the things of time.

I can not say "*AMEN*" if I do not also add, "cost what it may". For to **PRAY THIS PRAYER HONESTLY WILL COST EVERYTHING.**

---Anonymous---

APPENDIX VI
ANNUAL SELF-EVALUATION

Give every **YES** answer 5 points, every **NO** answer 0. If your score is 95 to 100, you have already put on immortality!!! 85 to 90, you have already reach perfection! 65 to 80, you are an asset in the work of the kingdom! 45 to 60 you are making progress. 25 to 40, you may be in a category called <u>carnal</u> or <u>feebleminded</u>. 0 to 20, GOD IS YET LONGSUFFERING.

1. Do you read your Bible more this year than last year?   Yes [ ] NO [ ]

2. Have you recently visited anyone in the hospital that was not a personal friend?   YES [ ] NO [ ]

3. If you visited the sick in home or hospital this year, did you pray for them and read the scripture?   YES [ ] NO [ ]

4. Have you paid your tithes faithfully all year?   YES [ ] NO [ ]

5. Did you fast at all this past year?   YES [ ] NO [ ]

6. Did you go on at least one three day consecration within the past year?   YES [ ] NO [ ]

7. Have you fasted more this year than last year?   YES [ ] NO [ ]

8. Are you faithful to week night services?   YES [ ] NO [ ]

9. Do you usually get to service in time for prayer?   YES [ ] NO [ ]

10. Did you start the prayer at anytime for any service within this last year?   YES [ ] NO [ ]

11. Have you visited any correctional facility for a service within the past year? YES [ ] NO [ ]

12. Have you made a special effort to assist or to support the needy lately? YES [ ] NO [ ]

13. Have you led one person to the Lord this past year? YES [ ] NO [ ]

14. Have you witnessed to one stranger this year? YES [ ] NO [ ]

15. Have you past one tract this year? YES [ ] NO [ ]

16. Do you attend Sunday School? YES [ ] NO [ ]

17. Do you attend Bible Study at your own church? YES [ ] NO [ ]

18. Are you able to praise the Lord at all times, even in times of adversity? YES [ ] NO [ ]

19. Were you filled or refilled with the Holy Ghost within this past year? YES [ ] NO [ ]

20. Have you given at least one sacrificial offering (money you sorely needed) within this past year? YES [ ] NO [ ]

Total number YES responses _____

Multiplied by 5 _____

Total_____

Compare your total with the categories on the top of the previous page

APPENDIX VII
THE TRIPARTITE NATURE OF MAN

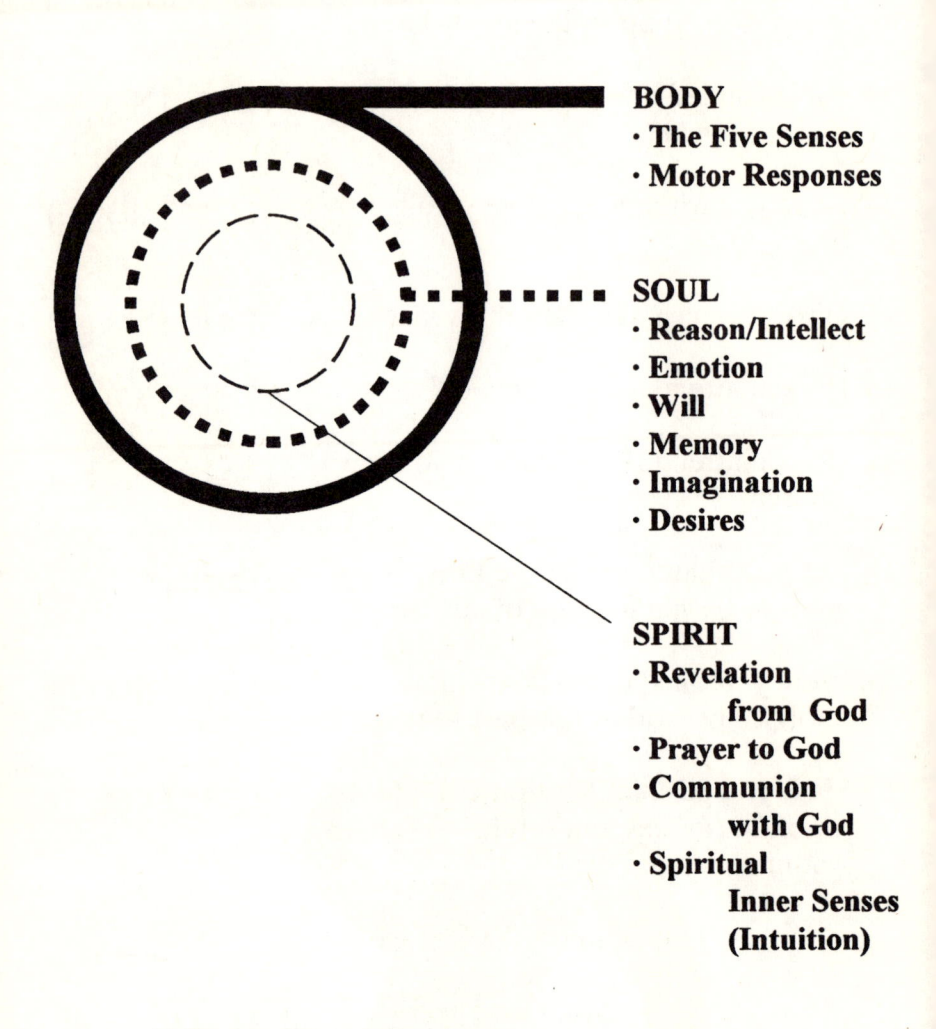

BODY
- **The Five Senses**
- **Motor Responses**

SOUL
- **Reason/Intellect**
- **Emotion**
- **Will**
- **Memory**
- **Imagination**
- **Desires**

SPIRIT
- **Revelation from God**
- **Prayer to God**
- **Communion with God**
- **Spiritual Inner Senses (Intuition)**

Diagramatic Relationship Between Body, Soul and Spirit

APPENDIX VII
THE TRIPARTITE NATURE OF MAN

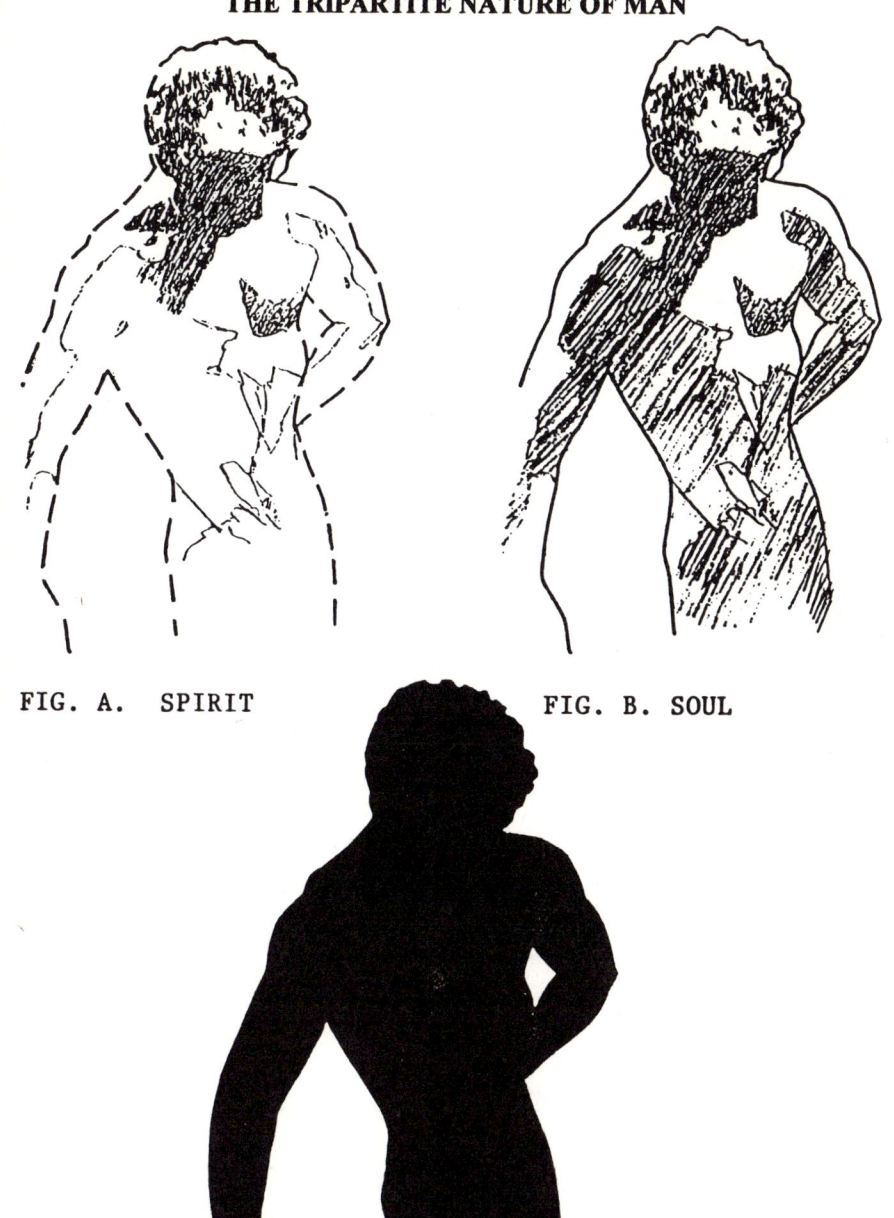

FIG. A. SPIRIT

FIG. B. SOUL

FIG. C. BODY

BIBLIOGRAPHY

THE HOLY BIBLE, Kings James Version

THE HOLY BIBLE, New International Version.

E.M. Bounds, THE POSSIBILITY OF PRAYER

Jerry Bridges, PURSUIT OF HOLINESS

Charles Erdman, THE EPISTLE OF PAUL TO THE EPHESIANS: An Exposition

Fay Ellis Butler, AFFLICTIONS, WHY ME?
AFTER DELIVERANCE, THEN WHAT?
REJECTION, THE RULING SPIRIT
THE SEDUCTION OF THE SAINTS

E.W. Kenyon, THE NAME OF JESUS

John D. Lawrence, SOUL WINNER'S INSTITUTE, Training You How to Work For God.

Andrew Murray, THE BLOOD OF THE CROSS
THE MINISTRY OF INTERCESSION

Watchman Nee, THE SPIRITUAL MAN

Jesse Penn-Lewis, WAR ON THE SAINTS

Strong's, EXHAUSTIVE CONCORDANCE OF THE BIBLE

W.E. Vine, et al, VINE'S EXPOSITORY DICTIONARY OF BIBLICAL WORDS

OTHER BOOKS BY THE AUTHOR

SEDUCTION OF THE SAINTS. (#100) If you do not understand satan's subtle plan to destroy you and your church, you may fall because of false prophecies and false ministries. 'Seducing Spirits' work well with 'spiritual blindness', 'spiritual ignorance', and 'spiritual complacency'. **$4.00**

AFTER DELIVERANCE, THEN WHAT? (#101) Satan never stops! Even after your deliverance, he will attempt to oppress you with the same 'unclean spirits' and/or your past. You are only 'more than a conqueror' if you understand the warfare and fight. **$4.00**

AFFLICTIONS: WHY ME? (#102) As long as we live in this world, we will have problems. The author identifies the kinds of afflictions the believer experiences, (e.g., social physical, spiritual, mental,etc.) it causes, manifestations, solutions, remedies and offers prevention, healing, endurance, with Biblical and medical documentation. **$4.00**

REFLECTIONS OF A CHURCH MAN: REV RALPH N. ELLIS, CHURCH OF GOD IN CHRIST 1922-1990. (#103) Rev. Ellis, sick and dying in 1922, went to Memphis, heard the gospel preached by Charles Harrison Mason, accepted Christ, was healed and called to preach. Read about Rev. Ellis' first-hand experience in the early church; his account of 69 years in the C.O.G.I.C; the teachings of Bishop Mason, the early church organization, and compare and contrast the differences and/or similarities with the early church and the church today. **$3.00**

HOW TO BE HOLY, HAPPY AND HEALTHY. (#104) This book discusses the interrelationship of health, happiness and holiness; explaining how stress produces distress, which results in diseases and spiritual affliction. **$3.00**

REJECTION, THE RULING SPIRIT (#105) Did you know that all cultures have 'a ruling spirit'? Read to know about 'ruling spirits' manifest themselves in our personal and spiritual lives, and how satan uses it/them to magnify feelings of <u>inferiority, defeat and worthlessness.</u> After reading this book, you will understand your actions as well as those around you. **$4.00**

HOW TO MINISTER TO THE SEXUALLY ABUSED. (#106) It is estimated that a minimum of 25% of all women in this country have been sexually abused and most of them never reported. This work gives an overview of the problem, explaining what takes places mentally and spiritually when the victim is abused--how there is demonic transference when such abuse occurs. Read the Biblical reference of how to be free and delivered from the thoughts, memories and dreams resulting from such abuse. **$4.00**

HOW TO MINISTER TO THE SEXUALLY ABUSED.(#106) It is estimated that a minimum of 25% of all women in this country have been sexually abused and most of them never reported. This work gives an overview of the problem, explaining what takes places mentally and spiritually when the victim is abused--how there is demonic transference when such abuse occurs. Read the Biblical reference of how to be free and delivered from the thoughts, memories and dreams resulting from such abuse. **$4.00**

WHY ARE GOD'S PEOPLE SICK? (#107) Find out why believers are taking as much medicines as non-believers, and visiting the doctor as much as those not professing salvation. The author addresses the issues of not adhering to I Peter 5:7, and Philippians 4:6. **$3.00**

HOPE FOR HOMOSEXUALS. (#108) Homosexuals in and out of the church are candidates for deliverance. Read this book to learn of the origins of homosexuality, its manifestations, cure (Bible-based), and methods of deliverance and counseling. (A must reading for all church workers, counselors and ministers.) **$4.00**

THE SHAPE YOU'RE IN: THE USES OF NUTRITIONAL THERAPY. (#109) Read this and become enlightened concerning your diet, disease and how most of our illnesses, e.g. high blood pressure, cancer, heart disease can be traced to diet. Learn how to maintain good health through proper nutrition and vitamin therapy. **$3.00**

SHAPE UP: FOR WOMEN ONLY. (#110) The incidence and prevalence of PMS, cramps, 'hot flashes', and cancers are increasing. This book discusses the why's and gives the reader options and solutions. **$2.00**

IMPORTANT NEWS:FOR MEN ONLY (#117) Male Impotence, cancer of the prostrate and other male organs are on the increase. This book discusses causes, prevention and cure. **$2.00**

OVERWEIGHT? GET THE FACTS.(#111) Look around you!!! Diets fail. Read this book to get the facts on how to control your weight sensibly. **$1.00**

HOW TO MINISTER TO CHRISTIANS IN BONDAGE.
(#114) This work will open up your understanding to the way satan attacks the mind, spirit and body. The book will enable the reader to recognize and deal with the 'spirits of oppression' and 'depression' and how to be delivered from bondage and ways to avoid bondage. **$4.00**

RIGHTS, REWARDS, RESPONSIBILITIES.
(#116) This book discusses the basic principles that God expects us to adhere to: not being ignorant of satan's devices, controlling your tongue, the language of prayer and God's response, etc. **$3.00**

****

ABOUT THE AUTHOR

FAY ELLIS BUTLER, raised in the Church of God in Christ, is the daughter of a pastor, the late Rev. Ralph N. Ellis, and the wife of a pastor, Rev. John L. Butler, who is also a practicing attorney in New York. A product of the New York City Public Schools, FAY is a Registered Nursed, received her Masters Degrees from Columbia University and her Ph.D. in Medical Anthropology from Columbia University in 1982. A mother of six children, a teacher, a scholar and an anointed evangelist, she uses her talents to work with and for people, traveling extensively as an evangelist, lecturer, counselor and workshop leader. Her favorite scripture "I can do all things through Christ which strengtheneth me" (Phil 4.13) enables her to fulfill her call to 'work while it is day'.

****

TO ORDER:
Add 15% for POSTAGE AND HANDLING
MAIL CHECK OR MONEY ORDER TO:
Dr. Fay Ellis Butler
P.O. Box 330702, Stuyvesant Station
Brooklyn, NY 11233

ORDER FORM

Dr. Fay Ellis Butler
Ellis-Butler Ministries
PO Box 330702, Stuyvesant Station
Brooklyn, NY 11233

Book #	Name of Book	# of Copies	$Price ea.	Total

SUB TOTAL $ _____

Add 15% Postage & Handling $ _____

TOTAL COST
(Amt. Enclosed) $ _____

Mail Check or Money Order payable to: Dr. Fay Ellis Butler and mail to address above.

Your Name _____

Address _____

Tele _____